An Endorsement of ***Destined for a Mission*** from
Dan Davis, founding pastor of
HOPE Chapel, Austin, Texas

I have known Herman Neusch and Kathy Glover both for over 20 years, although their friendship with each other is fairly recent. I served as pastor in their respective churches over the years and know them both as having proven character, a zest for life, and a deep love for Jesus.

Herman is amazing! He is the real Indiana Jones, but has invaded far more venues of engagement, including government service, business ventures, and humanitarian aid. Somehow, through this range of activity, his passion for Christ and love for his family has been unabated. At an age when almost all of his contemporaries have faded from the scene, Herman discovered the despair and hopelessness of the Haitian people. As with everything else in his life, he has gone far beyond the tourist's excitement in seeing a new place, or the academic's attempt to study and understand. He has thrown himself into the seemingly impossible task of bringing hope to the poorest people in our part of the world.

Wherever Herman goes, there is a vortex of energy and activity that attracts all in his path. This has characterized his amazing life story that Kathy Glover has faithfully recounted. Herman's passion for Christ and for mission continues strong and vibrant.

Destined for a Mission:
The Life Journey of Herman Neusch

As told to Kathy Glover

ISBN 13: 978-0-9820141-4-1
ISBN 10: 0-9820141-4-7

Produced in 2009 in the United States of America
as a service from Simple Publishing,
a divison of Woolstrum Publishing House, LLC.

www.simplepublishing.com

16 15 14 13 12 11 10 09 08 07 06 05 04 03 02 01

*I dedicate this book to my precious wife, Janet, for
all her patience and assistance in gathering the
information and to our Heavenly Father who has
blessed me so mightily my entire life.*

Herman

*I would like to dedicate this book to my family:
to Danny, for your patience during
the book writing process
to Shelby, for your creative flare and
unique perspectives
to Shannon, who was quite inspired for a
season by Christian biographies.
You have reminded me that there is always room
for one more good story.*

Kathy

Table of Contents

"We proclaim to you what we have seen and heard, so that you may also have fellowship with us."
I John 1:3

Introduction
Take My Hand

I WILL TAKE HOLD OF YOUR HAND.
ISAIAH 42:6

I am a man on a mission. You will find that my mission has changed over time. Through the years, I have traveled to many states in the U.S. and to a multitude of foreign nations. I made and lost a fortune, married three times, and raised six cherished children. I have met with leaders known to history, served my country in the military during wartime, and have become an advocate for one of the poorest countries in the world.

I know these many accomplishments did not come as a result of my great abilities or by random circumstances. As I look back on the events of my life, I know it is God who has woven them together. Proverbs 16:9 says, "In his heart a man plans his course, but the Lord determines his steps."

Now I am on a mission to help the hungry in Haiti. I hope you will join me in that effort. Ultimately, my mission is to know God and make Him known.

In the pages of this book, I speak openly about the events of my life and about my spiritual journey. Wherever you are in your own journey, please take my hand through these pages and walk with me awhile. I invite you into my story and I hope that as you travel along my path, it helps you along your own.

Everyone believes something; every human being has some sort of faith, whether specifically defined or more general. That means, in many ways, that we are all on a mission to know Truth. I believe we are not left to wander through life wondering about Truth. Once we begin looking for Truth, we find it is a person: Jesus Christ. He does not leave us to our own thoughts, but guides us in many ways: through God's Word, the Bible; through His Church, with centuries of good teaching; and through His Holy Spirit.

I humbly ask all my readers to consider the Truth of Christ. We know it is a historical fact that He walked upon the earth and was killed on a cross. Believers in every generation have known him as the resurrected Lord and Savior. If there is anything stirring in you that says there is more to life than just what we see, let me say that it is God calling you to walk with Him. Will you take His hand?

I invite you to consider the highest mission in life: to know God and to serve where He leads you. Come join me on the best possible mission!

Author's note

I believe that not all characters are in books. Some people are greater than any author's imagination or artful work of fiction. Before I met Herman Neusch, I knew he was no average retiree. I had to wait for him to return from Alaska to meet him, before he went off traveling again. The first thing I noticed was the steely glint in his eyes that speaks of fierce determination. I learned that he is a man who gets things done, and he is seldom deterred for any length of time.

What I find inspiring about Mr. Neusch is that he does not disqualify himself from rising to a task. He did not do so growing up poor in the Texas Panhandle, nor does he do so now as an octogenarian. I would add that his determination is tempered by Holy Spirit-inspired humility. He is, at once, a formidable character and a truly grateful person. I am very grateful for the opportunity to help him tell his story.

Kathy Glover

Chapter One
Mission: The Hungry in Haiti

RICH AND POOR HAVE THIS IN COMMON:
THE LORD IS THE MAKER OF THEM ALL.
PROVERBS 22:2

The phone rang. It was my neighbor, Art Wood. "Herman," he said, "I have something you might like to see."

"What's that?" I asked, not admitting that the call was a distraction from my guests.

"A solar cooker!" Art replied.

"Ok," I said with a mild curiosity. "Bring it over."

My friends, the Winters, were visiting to tell me about their charitable work in Haiti. They had been several times to the island nation and had come to my house to introduce me to their friend Eddie Francois, who serves as a pastor in Haiti.

Of all days, Art picked that day to show me his new interest. When he arrived and showed us his contraption, Eddie went bonkers. I mean the fellow got so excited he was uncontainable.

"This could save my nation!"

Something stirred inside of me as I realized how divine intervention was at work at that very moment at my house in Burnet, Texas. You could say that I was watching the birth of a great mission.

Mission Defined

A mission is defined as an operational task; someone is given an assignment to complete for the benefit of others. I can honestly say that I have often felt that call and proceeded to complete the task with a certain amount of zeal. I think I was just wired that way. Things need to be done and I might as well help.

Haiti is a perfect example. Haiti is in desperate need. Not desperate like we think of in the United States when the stock market takes a nosedive and our portfolios are worth less than a few days before. No, children are starving in Haiti; we hear reports that children are given cooked mud to help stave off their hunger. Food prices increased as much as 100% in 2008 alone. Unemployment reached 80% years ago and remains there. There is simply no work available that results in payment. The government and businesses are plagued by flagrant abuses and corruption. Haiti is by far the poorest nation in the western hemisphere.

Add to these issues the common practice of cutting trees for making charcoal. With the majority of the trees gone, the devastated land cannot hold its topsoil. This prompts mudslides every time a tropical storm or hurricane sweeps through the area.

On that fateful day in the year 2000 at my house in central Texas, far from the debilitating poverty of Haiti, here came Art and his solar cooker. Pastor Eddie Francois and Lee and Elizabeth Winter watched Art's demonstration and realized the potential for helping Haitians cook without cutting more trees. We learned that a solar cooker can be used like any oven; it just takes longer to cook. It seemed extremely important. So I took up the cause with great enthusiasm and raised money to buy and ship solar cookers.

Soon, I was put in contact with Lowell Yoder, a gentleman from Ohio. He also had a mission related to Haiti. Lowell had helped build more than 100 churches there. He bought into the idea of the solar cookers, and we joined forces in raising support.

To my dismay, we discovered that the corruption on the island would be an enormous obstacle. There was no way to get the shipment passed customs short of paying a huge bribe. That meant that our valuable commodities would be stalled indefinitely. I could not bear the thought of the cookers sitting in a port warehouse, never to be used. So I quit asking for money for this cause and decided to wait and see what would come of it all.

Mission Refined

Out of the blue one day, I received a phone call from the U.S. Embassy in Port-au-Prince. Kennedy Veal, a cultural attaché, had found me!

"I hear you want to send solar cookers down here."

"Well, yes, I did, but getting through customs is a big problem," I confessed.

"I can arrange for you to send them through the U.S. Embassy. Send them directly to me. I can get them in." Mr. Veal sounded certain.

Believe me, I went back to work with renewed zeal. Just think, I did not call the Embassy, they called me!

Soon Lowell and I were able to buy two hundred solar cookers. Mr. Veal called back to finalize the plans for the shipment.

"Aren't you coming, too?" I had not planned to go.

"I suppose I can go for a few days," I said. I looked into travel plans.

Lowell called to say that he was going too. I told him I was only staying a few days.

"Oh, that's no good," he said. "We need to go for two weeks." We decided to take the man who built the cookers along with us and set out for two weeks in Haiti.

I found that Lowell was right. I needed to stay in the country longer than a few days, but what I saw broke my heart.

The Mission Begins

We were met in grand fashion in the Caribbean. On our first evening, Lowell and I were whisked away to a private home surrounded by a stonework fence. There were armed guards outside and many well-dressed people of means inside. We were treated to every luxury. The next day the Chamber of Commerce put on a huge promotion complete with a special ceremony, a reception and plenty of media coverage.

Representatives from other embassies were invited and we demonstrated how the solar cookers could be used to prepare a traditional Haitian meal. To say the least, the cookers and our party from the

U.S. were well received. For the rest of our stay, I had a chance to find out more about this land of contrasts.

The Land of Mountains

Upon arrival, a visitor might think that Haiti is a tropical paradise. The light-colored sand beaches give way to sharply rising hillsides that become mountains. Brilliant flowers show off their colorful blossoms. Nice homes nestle into the hills. Typical of the Caribbean, the waters around Haiti are a vivid blue and feature coral reefs that support a variety of fish. The early inhabitants called the island Ayiti, which means "land of mountains." And so it is. No larger than the State of Maryland, Haiti has four large ranges. It is the most mountainous of the islands that form a chain in the northern Caribbean Sea. Some of the peaks reach over 8,700 feet.

The western side of Haiti has two peninsulas, one north and one south. They give the map a horseshoe shape or the look of a backwards C. To the East, Haiti shares the island of Hispaniola with the Dominican Republic. While the people in the DR speak Spanish, Haiti has French roots and the people speak Creole. Over 8.3 million people live in Haiti, which sits on one third of the island.

What might appear a paradise is not so, on closer inspection. The mahogany trees, exported to make fine furniture, no longer grow there. The land and the sea have been over-harvested and the once productive island cannot feed itself. Even the topography presents a challenge; torrential rains, up to 145 inches a year, wash away crops in the south, while the northern side of the island is arid, receiving as little as 5 inches of rain a year.

The same mountains that make pretty views also make road building difficult. Transportation is a time-consuming adventure in Haiti. I know from personal experience that it can take two hours to travel 20 miles. There are car-sized potholes that a vehicle dips into, disappearing from view, until it can crawl back up the other side. It is reported that only 20% of the roads are paved, and most of those are near Port-au-Prince, the capital city. That means rural travel is quite challenging.

Past and Present

Haiti's early history might sound promising. The land once supported a French colony of plantations that grew coffee, sugar and bananas. The fishing industry was prolific and the hardwood forests were thick.

One of the few successful slave rebellions in history took place there. In the 1790's, the African slaves brought over to work the plantations vastly outnumbered the French slave owners. They revolted and gained their independence from France in 1804. The former slaves established a democracy, only the second one in the western hemisphere. Yet freedom never flourished. Haiti has been subject to tyranny, military dictators and poverty ever since. The instability is so great that, in one ten month period, Haiti saw the rise and fall of six governments.

In this land of contrast, there are few wealthy people; most Haitians are devastatingly poor. The streets of the cities are lined with peddlers trying to make a penny. The flowering plants and painted homes of Port-au-Prince give way to the cardboard houses of the poor. Sources claim that the capital city has fifty slums surrounding it, and that the population of the slums is greater than the city itself, estimated to be 1.3 million in 2007. The largest slum is Cite Soliel, a sprawling shantytown with open sewers and tens of thousands of children.

Dark Forces

The slaves brought tribal practices that have been mixed with parts of the Christian faith. Vodou, known in the U.S. as voodoo, is now a recognized religion in Haiti. Although it may look like mere superstition and colorful cultural ceremonies, followers of Vodou call upon spirits to possess them.

There is widespread belief in the story that the leaders of the slave revolt, centuries ago, dedicated Haiti to the Devil in return for winning independence from France. Although it may sound like a legend, it was taken seriously enough by President Aristide to attempt to renew the dedication during the country's 200th anniversary celebration in 2004. Reports say that a sudden outbreak of lightning at the dedication site prevented the ceremony from taking place.

It is my firm belief that this spiritual darkness encourages the turmoil and poverty that haunts Haiti today.

Storms of Two Kinds

Adding to the troubles are violent hurricanes. The storms typically come up on the southwest side of the island, threatening people, wiping out crops, and prompting mudslides. In 1963, Hurricane Flora killed 8,000 people. In 2004, Hurricane Jeanne flooded most of the country, leaving 3,000 dead and tens of thousands homeless. In 2008, perhaps the worst year of all, four tropical storms and hurricanes hit in rapid succession: Fay, Gustav, Hannah and Ike. The degree of devastation is hard to grasp. Waist high rivers of mud and water washed away everything in their path. International aid came from many sources, yet the consequences of the '08 storms will remain for years.

The other storm so prevalent in Haiti is the political kind. The country has a long history of tyrannical dictators, enforcing their will upon the people by violence. UN Peacekeeping Forces have returned to Haiti many times and are currently quite visible, traveling the streets in sand colored vehicles, armed and ready. They were on hand in the spring of 2008 when food shortages and inflation brought people into the streets ready to riot over the price of rice.

Armed Guards

Crime is horrific in Haiti. On one of my earliest trips, I needed bolts for some small project I was working on. I walked over to the nearest little hardware store and was met by an armed guard at the entrance. He looked me over and decided I could be let in. As the door closed behind me, I found myself in a small room with another armed guard. I had to gain his permission as well, just for my simple little purchase. I did not feel particularly threatened by their presence, but it certainly made a point. Even small shop owners in the middle of the day are potential targets, so they do whatever they can to deter theft.

Humanity in the Chaos

Despite these horrendous obstacles, one thing struck me as I traveled around Haiti; these people are resilient. They make the most of very little. I saw children who were barely clothed, playing. They may have had a shirt or perhaps pants, but certainly not shoes. Some had no clothes at all. Yet they played; with sticks, with pebbles, or with an old bike tire. We found that a bag of rubber bands was a great treat for them. Kids would line up to get one and run off to play with this new commodity.

I found the adults to be amazingly open and approachable. Haitians are willing to connect with strangers. Whether you visit large cities or little villages, or merely pass people on the road, they will look at you. Despite all their poverty and hunger, they are willing to make eye contact and often smile. The smiles light up their faces in a compelling way.

I was so moved by this that I intentionally looked for responses when I returned to the U.S.

I flew into the Miami airport and looked for people who would make eye contact with me. There were hundreds of people coming and going that day, perhaps thousands. Yet I found that only one person returned my gaze. For all our wealth in America, we do not see people. Despite the fact that they have nothing, the Haitians acknowledge fellow human beings. This has stirred something in my soul since my first visit.

The Mission Advances

There is much more to my story of Haiti. You may see, as I do, that the circumstances have come together in an amazing way. The parts of the story really do seem woven by a master plan. To this day, I am still amazed that my neighbor just happened to arrive with a solar cooker, of all things, on the very day that a pastor from a terribly poor country was visiting my house! The story has developed to include many wonderful folks from Texas to Massachusetts and South Dakota. Toss in a great deal of prayer, a dried food processing company and a gardening program. It is a story that includes hunger, agriculture and advocacy.

Now, I know a thing or two about agriculture. In fact, I know something about hunger as well. And some might say that advocacy is my middle name. So I suppose it is not a surprise that I am dedicated to this mission to feed the hungry in Haiti. Let me tell you how the pieces to this puzzle have all come together to make me a man on a mission.

Chapter Two
Humble Beginnings

WHO DESPISES THE DAY OF SMALL THINGS?
ZECHARIAH 4:10

I grew up poor. I am telling you, Dust Bowl poor. My teenage mother gave birth to me on December 20, 1924 in St. Francis, Texas, a tiny community twelve miles east of Amarillo with nothing much there but a Catholic Church and a filling station. Times were hard in those days, but as I look back, I can see how God provided for me and protected me from the very beginning.

The truth is my parents married about two months before I was born. Even that simple fact amazes me. My mother, Louise Huseman, was 17 and my father, William Neusch, was 29. I am grateful to God that my mother did not have an abortion. Although it was illegal at the time, she may have felt desperate enough to look into that option. I am thankful that she did not. I also want to give credit to my father for marrying my mother and for raising me. I came to know him as a kindhearted man. I see how that was true regarding his decision to marry my mother and raise many children.

For three or four years we lived with my father's parents. This may have been primarily for economic reasons, but I suspect it helped my young mother with the duties of child raising. The stories are told that Granddad could often be found outside, taking a nap, with me curled up on top of him. There was the time he encouraged me to reach up for the milk bucket that Grandma had placed on the counter. He got on his knees and pretended to reach for it. Although I was just a toddler, I followed his example and was successful in pulling it down, spilling the milk everywhere. Granddad thought this was terribly funny. Grandma, however, did not.

Protection

One of the earliest stories I was told about occurred when I was an infant. My parents took me with them to a dance in their Model T. It began to rain, and they decided to return home. In those days cars did not have headlights, so they had a head-on collision with a vehicle coming the other way. I was thrown through the windshield and found in a field, unharmed. I consider that one of the first of many miracles.

This harsh area I grew up in is called the Llano Estacado. This parched, flat land is marked by gently sloping draws and occasional canyons. It has dramatic sweeping views, extending toward the horizon. The Panhandle is known for fierce winds and dry land. Water had always been the critical issue there, but better pumping technology came along in the 1920's and several small towns flourished.

The area was especially dry in the beginning of the 1930's with more drought conditions to come. It could be tempting for some folks to say that miracles were in short supply back in the dusty days of the Texas Panhandle. I would say there were no luxuries, but there was provision.

My dad bought a piece of land outside of Sunray, Texas, which is about 50 miles north of Amarillo and a bit east of Dumas. Dad had a team of horses and a wagon deliver materials so he could build a two-room shack. The family moved in, and he set out to be a wheat farmer. Dad bought the land and a tractor on time, but it never rained, and he never harvested a single grain of wheat.

The railroad company asked permission to lay tracks through our property, and he granted it. The first train that came through stopped at our house. Two men got out, started up Dad's tractor, and loaded it on the train. It had been repossessed. After that, we lived by picking up empty bottles on the side of the road and selling them to bootleggers. You could say that put us in the recycling business early on! This gave us a few coins to buy flour and .22 bullets. The ammunition helped us gain a meager dinner and thin out the jackrabbit population at the same time. Even in those lean years, God provided for us.

Tough Times, Tumbleweeds and a Tornado

The dust storms of that time were fierce. As a child, I did not know much about the Dust Bowl and the Black Blizzards in the Great Plains, but I knew firsthand about terrible dust blowing through Texas. The tumbleweeds would blow against the fence, and dust would fill them to the point that the cows could walk right up over the fence! We would go to bed with a sheet over us like a tent. In the morning, there would be at least a half an inch of dust weighing down the sheet.

The fine, silty stuff was unavoidable on the worst days. I recall one day in particular; it started out clear, but you could watch the sky turn black. A thick darkness came down on us from the North. Once the dust storm hit, you could hardly see a thing. The best we could do was to run inside, but our house certainly could not keep out the dust. It blew through every crack and cranny. I wasn't aware that we were living in historic times, but apparently there were stories in the news about the worst dust storm. It hit the Texas Panhandle hard in mid-April of 1935. As a kid, I didn't know or care about making the newspaper; I just grew tired of the dust.

With no farm equipment left, my Dad moved that little shack into the town of Sunray, and that is where I started school. One day, the school kids were telling tales of a tornado that had swept through town. I ran home to tell my parents, but they sent me back to school, disbelieving my fantastic story. However, the account was true. A tornado had picked up a house with two men in it on one side of Sunray and had carried that house completely across town. One of those men jumped out of the house, some way or another, and was saved. The other man was killed when the house crashed to the ground.

The blowing dust in the spring and summer was bad enough, but in the winter, the wind blew in ice. The cold rain would freeze as it fell and then collect on the wire fences and power lines. There would be balls of ice surrounding the metal barbs on the fence wires. Sometimes the telephone lines were so heavily coated with ice, they would snap the poles and send them crashing down. I heard that a man in a taxi in Amarillo had an ice-incrusted telephone pole fall on the back of his vehicle. Had he not been sitting up front, he surely would have died.

Then there was the wind. It was as if it gained speed and grew colder as it swept out of the North on bone-chilling days. My dad would tell us "the only thing between Amarillo and the North Pole was a barbed wire fence with two strands down!" It sure didn't do much to block that cold wind.

Diversions Among the Chores

Life was pretty tough in those days, and people were not so concerned about kids having fun. There were not a great many diversions, but I do remember that we had a sizable stock tank out by the windmill, and on the hottest days we would get into that tank. I don't think you could say any of us really learned to swim.

My dad was a short, strong man who loved his children. He would take my brother Arnold and me out in the evenings and teach us how to play baseball. In our elementary school years he coached our team. At one point we were good enough to play against a Catholic high school team and we won! I am pretty sure there was some amount of good luck involved in that victory, but I like to give credit to my dad's coaching ability.

Mother was always busy with the girls and there were plenty of those in my family. After me and Arnold, Mom had five girls and one more boy: Rita, Myrtle, Zona, Rosemary, Betty and Ralph. Just doing laundry for that many of us was a huge job. We hauled water in buckets from the windmill to the house to heat in a tank on the stove. Then the heated water went into an old style washer. This was an arduous process, so it was not done all that often. I can remember dirty clothes piling up in our room and delving into the heap to find the cleanest item to wear.

As I look back, I believe the Lord used the experiences of my childhood to prompt in me great compassion for people who live without the basics like sufficient food and clean water. Even then, He was weaving the pieces of my life together.

My brother Arnold and I weren't just close in age, we were friends. We hunted rabbits and went fishing together. Arnold tells the story of going on a picnic near Canyon, Texas, when we were very young and breaking a twig off a tree to serve as a fishing pole. We tied a string on it and bent a straight pin for a hook. We put a worm on it and caught some blue gill perch. We didn't require fancy gear, just opportunity.

Fishing was important to me in those days and has been a favorite pastime ever since. Growing up in the dry plains, my dad used to say that the Amarillo area was "the center of the very best fishing in the country; three hundred miles that direction and three hundred miles in the other." We were lucky enough to live right in the center!

Dad had his way of showing his affection to us, but you couldn't say there was a great deal of nurturing in those days. He made a point of taking his children to the Catholic Church every Sunday. Mother did not go, but the rest of us sure did. One year, as Easter approached, I heard kids talking about the Easter Rabbit coming to bring eggs. All my younger siblings were excited about this, and truthfully, so was I. We decided we wanted to set up some nests and hoped that Rabbit would bring us some colored eggs too. Our parents tried to discourage us from doing this, but we did it anyway. It moved them so much that they insisted we put them out the next night as well. In the morning, we had Easter eggs!

The Widow's Help

By the first grade, the schoolboys had started boxing each other at recess. I could handle my own pretty well except for two boys who were sons of a widow lady. For some reason, they had me scared to death.

One time they told me that their mom wanted me to go home with them. I was afraid not to go along, and when we passed by my little brother, I motioned for him to come, too. When we got there, she brought us out a big sack of groceries because she knew how poor we were. I hate to admit this, but we were so fearful of the boys, we thought they had poisoned the food. We buried that bag of groceries and never said a word to our parents. I felt so bad for that poor widow since my parents never once acknowledged her generosity.

On the other hand, it might be just as well that we didn't show up with groceries from a neighbor. I remember the day a government man arrived with bags of groceries. There was a new assistance program and we received the benefits. My mother bawled as much as I can ever recall. She was so embarrassed to think the government had to help her feed her family, but shortly after Mother's big cry, the rest of us sure enjoyed everything that grocery man brought us.

On the Ranch

Employment was scarce, and when Dad got an offer to work on a ranch, he packed up the family and we all moved out west of Amarillo for a year or so. There was a mare on the ranch that was gentle enough to ride without a saddle. We were still small and would lead her up by the wooden fence to scramble on her back.

One time, there were horses and mules out in a pasture and Dad asked Arnold to bring them in. He obeyed, riding out on the mare. As the herd headed toward the barn between two sections of fence, the horses picked up speed until they were running full tilt. As the mare galloped faster, Arnold shifted further forward a bit at a time until he fell off, flipping right over the horse's head. She came to quick halt. He was lying on the ground, between her front legs, looking up at her. This scared him so badly that he never got on a horse again. This could have been a serious tragedy, but he did not even get hurt. You see, once again, God was at work, protecting a kid on a horse.

School Days

When it came time for school again, Dad sent me to live with Mother's parents so I could attend a public school near St. Francis. My cousin lived there too, and we drove a one-horse buggy to school. By the next school year, my family had all moved to St. Francis and the Catholic school had opened. My school-aged siblings and I would walk a mile or so to our neighbors the Bertrands' house and then ride with them to school. By the time we returned with them and walked back home, it had been quite a long day. I don't remember a great deal about my school days, but I do recall that walk each morning and afternoon.

One particular assignment that does stand out in my memory was when the nuns directed us to tell our parents we loved them before we returned to school the next day. This was not a natural thing in our home. We had forgotten this and gone to bed when all of the sudden, three of us remembered the charge the nuns had given. We got up and were whispering.

"You tell 'em."

"No, you tell 'em."

At this time we all lived in a four-room house. Our parents were in bed, but they could hear us and they asked, "What are you kids doing up?"

One of us got the nerve to say, "We love you."

They responded, "Oh, be quiet and go to bed."

Blackbird Pie and Rabbit Stew

Being hungry can make you resourceful. One of many days when there was no food in the house, Mother suggested we shoot blackbirds because that was one thing we had in abundance. My dad and brother and I went out on a particular day when there was a whole flock of blackbirds perched on a fence. Dad shot, but only hit a few. He was pretty discouraged because it took a number of blackbirds to feed our whole family. I saw many birds out in a field feeding, and I asked him if I could try to get some.

"Sure," he said. "Take the shotgun."

Just at the moment when I got up close to the blackbirds, here came a hawk that swooped down toward them. Those little blackbirds all tried to take cover under a tumbleweed, so I shot at them and left the ground covered with dead birds. The surviving blackbirds started up again, trying to escape, but here came the hawk. Once again, the blackbirds tried to hide under another tumbleweed. I shot again with more success.

Dad, who didn't realize my intended target, came running across the field. "Quit shooting at that stupid hawk!" he hollered.

We had plenty of blackbirds for pie that evening.

Unfortunately, there were times that we did not even have coins for shotgun shells. On those occasions, Arnold and I went out with rocks and caught some young jackrabbits. The younger ones try to hide and you can get pretty close to them. We were successful enough for Mother to cook rabbit stew from time to time.

On some evenings, we would have a chicken for dinner if we were lucky enough to have any to raise. Those were the days when you had to catch one, ring its neck, and pull the feathers off before you could cook it. Dad would ask for "the part that flew over the fence last." The kids would ask for the tender gizzard, but with so many children, some of us found bones in the "gizzard" we were served.

To be honest, there were times we had nothing to eat, perhaps a bit of flour and water to make thin gravy. Being hungry leaves an impression. The hunger may be addressed later, but that experience does not leave you. In my case, I believe the Lord used that hunger to place in me great compassion for the poor all over the world. I can relate to them. I have gone to sleep hungry, too.

Working Hard and Growing Up

One summer I was offered a job by a neighbor with a two-horse team and a go-devil; a system to cut the weeds out from among the corn. He paid me fifty cents a day to work all day long. Since work was hard to come by and I was the oldest of eight children, I gave my folks all of the fifty-cent pieces I made that summer. I had decided to keep one for myself and buy candy when we went into town, but it was clear that they needed every bit of the money I could earn, so I surrendered that one as well. I don't think that was because I was so gracious or kind, but more that the Lord was working a practical sense of responsibility in me. It was clear that we had needs, and that I could do something about them.

This has become an underlying principle that God has placed deep in me. It affects how I see others in need and my response to them. Quite simply, hard work is a valuable teacher and I can say that I've learned quite a bit.

In later years, Arnold and I went southwest of Amarillo to Nazareth, Texas, to herd sheep in the summer months with my Granddad and Uncle Jakey. One day, a tired worker decided he would lie down in the pasture. He was enjoying a nap when a ground squirrel ran up his pants leg! We saw him move faster than we'd ever seen him go, and I learned that it is wise to pay attention. There is no napping on the job, even when tending sheep.

I worked one summer for my Aunt Katie for a dollar a day, and another summer I worked for a farmer for three dollars a day. I drove a truck out to the combines that were harvesting wheat. The harvesters filled my truck, and then I would take it to the granary and scoop all the wheat with a big shovel. It was quite a job. I recall finishing sixteen truckloads in one day.

During my senior year of high school, my Granddad and I were the only employees of a little dairy. We had twenty-one cows we had to milk by hand twice a day, so we were up at 4 a.m. This prompted falling asleep in class. In fact, I struggled in all of my classes except Shop. When I was dog tired the next morning, Granddad would say,

"C'mon, Herman, we've got to make a showing." I saw how important it is to take responsibilities seriously, even when I was tired.

I worked enough that I decided to buy a car. I bought a Model A Ford from a Mexican man for five dollars, but gasoline cost several pennies a gallon and I could not afford that. So I traded the Ford back to the same man for a Jersey heifer calf, which was something my family really did need at the time.

The House the Pigs Built

As tired as I was from working at the dairy, I got involved with the 4-H Club at Amarillo High School and wanted to raise pigs. Sears and Roebuck Company donated six female pigs to the club, and students wrote essays to determine who would be awarded one to raise. I wrote two essays, one for me and one for Arnold, and both the essays won. It was our start in the pig business!

The local county agent knew how little money we had, and he went to the bank to sign a loan for me. This was a huge help; now I could buy grain to feed the pigs. I raised registered Spotted Poland China pigs. Those are the white ones with black spots.

Back then some of the farmers had trouble keeping their piglets safe. The little ones needed to stay with the sows, yet the huge mama pigs could easily roll onto the babies and crush them. I pondered this problem and thought of a simple solution. With the babies nestled near the barn wall, I put a board in place high enough to clear the little ones, yet it extended out far enough to block the adult pig when she rolled. She could only turn so far. The babies were safe and my herd grew. I won first place at the 4-H show.

Sometime later, I heard that the owner of the lumber company wanted to raise pigs, so I called on the man and showed him my herd of prizewinners, and we agreed to a trade. He gained my pigs and I got all of the materials needed to build my folks a home. We didn't have to hire a builder in those days; we gathered the family and some of the neighbors and went to work raising a house. The job could be done in a few weeks. Those pigs greatly benefited my family.

The Iron General

Our high school needed a public address system. World War II was going on, so the principal challenged the students to a scrap iron drive to raise money. The drive would aid the war effort and pay for a school PA system all at once. We would be given an honorary rank depending upon how much we could collect. Since my family lived in the country, I knew all the farmers out there and I knew they had scrap iron piles. I hopped on my bicycle and went to visit each one and told them how desperately the government needed their iron. Every single one of them donated! I could get high school students to gather the iron, but I needed a way to transport it. I went to the local Army base to ask for trucks and they agreed. We had an enormous pile that brought in plenty for the PA system. For my efforts, the principal dubbed me "The General." Little did I know what rank I would have soon after that.

By the end of 1942, not quite halfway through the school year, I had an argument with my mother and decided to join the Navy. My friend Clifton Wall said he wanted to go, too. Clifton was still seventeen, and I was going to turn eighteen in two days. At that time, a parent's signature was required for anybody under 18. We forged them, and were set to go to Oklahoma City that very afternoon!

I began to think about finishing high school. I had not been the best of students in my senior year, but I had come this far and wanted to find some way to get a diploma. I went to see the principal and asked him what I might do about finishing. He went off to confer with other members of the administration and returned to say, "Herman, we are going to grant you a diploma." There was still an entire semester to go, but I suppose he was inclined to look with favor on "The General." When my friend decided he would try the same tactic, the principal kicked him right out of the office. I left for the Navy right away, leaving West Texas behind and thinking I was prepared for new adventures. It was 1942, and I was on a mission to fight for my country.

Chapter Three
From General to Seaman

Wily Women and One Big Scare

Boot Camp in San Diego, California, included a series of tests for me and my fellow trainees to determine in what way we might best serve the Navy. That included a test for Morse code. I did well, well enough to be selected for Radio School in Boulder, Colorado. As many young men in the Navy did, I met some girls. One in particular caught my eye and we began to date. She let me know that she was open to the notion of promiscuity and we planned our next date. On that very weekend, she was not to be found! Her girlfriend said she had gone to California. Sometime later, I received a letter from her saying she did not feel it was right to lead me down that path. As disappointed as I was at the time, now I can see how God protected me.

That protection continued when I was shipped out to sea. About the time for graduation from radio school, the Navy solicited volunteers to go to New

Guinea. My friend Joe Thompson and I decided to accept the offer, and we were assigned to *The Roschambeau*. The ship had been a French luxury liner caught up in the war effort and turned into a troop carrier. The officers stressed how careful we had to be.

"If you fall off the ship, we cannot stop, and we will not stop to pick you up." The concern was that if such a large ship as ours stopped, we would be a target for a torpedo from a Japanese sub.

We were not equipped with sonar, so to avoid detection, we did not travel in straight lines. The passage to the Pacific took weeks as we zigzagged our way across the ocean. The liner-turned-carrier had been outfitted with a five inch gun on the stern, or tail end, of the ship that would be a grand deterrent to other ships and to submarines. One day, I decided to take a nap under the platform that stood about three feet high and held the gun in place. BOOM!

I jolted awake, knowing we had been torpedoed. I grabbed my life jacket and ran to jump ship. Just before I got to the edge, I heard hollering. The gunners had taken a practice shot, and now they were yelling at me not to jump. Fortunately, I was spared a dip in the ocean which would have cost me my life. The warning had been clear; the officers would not have stopped the ship to fish me out of the sea had I jumped.

Although I was safe, the ship's crew discovered that the gun was so powerful, it had pulled loose from the welds and bolts that held it to the platform. It had to be repaired before we encountered a battle.

We arrived at the newly constructed Navy radio base in Finchaven, New Guinea, on the northeastern coast of the island. The Army had battled the Japanese for the site over many months and had just recently secured it. Army soldiers continued to occupy the area, even though the Navy ran the radio base.

One of the comforts we were afforded was a priest who offered Mass every day. I did not know at the time the influence this had on me. After a year of service, seamen were given two weeks of R&R in Australia. Many of the guys came back with wild tales of their sexual exploits. God was at work in my heart, and when the time came for my two weeks, I turned it down. I know this was a wise decision and that the strength to make it had come from a higher source.

Atheists in Foxholes

When we first arrived on base, there were two fellows in our company who made it quite clear that they were atheists and were not about to be swayed from their position in the least. Although we did not see any immediate danger from the enemy, the Army soldiers encouraged us to dig foxholes. They had been there long enough to know the situation, but we did not listen, assuming it was good-natured teasing by one branch of the military at the expense of another. After two days and nights of quiet, we had not complied.

By the third night, here came Japanese planes dropping bombs, and I ended up in an Army-dug foxhole with both of those two men. As the bombs fell and the anti-air craft guns boomed in response, they hollered, "Neusch, teach us how to pray!" Believe me, they were quite serious. Being a Catholic, I taught them the Apostles' Creed and that was their introduction to the Christian faith!

Not long after that, us Navy fellows set to work on our own foxholes. These were not mere trenches, but hollowed out enough and reinforced so the overhang provided cover. This protected us from our own anti-aircraft guns that sent bits of shrapnel flying in all directions.

Dangers Big and Small

We were intrigued by our tropical locale. New Guinea stretches across the ocean between Australia and the Philippines. Its sandy beaches quickly turn into rocky coral topped with a thin layer of soil. The trees that grow in this coral base are massive. They have many roots extending outward and are comprised of a wood that is too heavy to float.

Just after some new men had arrived, a mighty wind blew up and sent one of these trees crashing into our tents. Two of the new Navy boys ran over to see what had happened, when suddenly, a second tree fell, killing them both. Sadly, this proved that we were not just in danger from enemy fire.

A small but real threat, at least for most us, came from disease-carrying mosquitoes. They were fast and thick on our island base. We had to use every defense we could, from bug repellents to netting over our cots. That is, everyone except Joe Thompson. My good friend from radio school seemed immune to mosquitoes. I never did find out why that was, but he never slept under a net, and to my knowledge, never suffered from bites, much less malaria.

Of course, the ever-present threat was the Japanese, who were tremendously fierce fighters.

Because of our remote location, there were very few lights, making it dark enough at night that the Navy personnel began to show movies on the beach. We had a screen set up with its back to the shoreline and logs placed in rows in front of the screen for seating. One night, a Japanese plane swooped down on us, no doubt drawn by the light of the movie projector. He came directly at us, toward the back of the screen from the ocean, and dropped a bomb at the edge of the water. I wasn't there that night, but I heard how fast our men scrambled to safety. Some were injured, but despite the close call, we did not suffer a single fatality. This just reinforced my firm belief that God watches over us and knows the length of our days.

Friend Lost and Friend Found

Before I left Texas, President Roosevelt employed the draft to call men to arms. One day I was out in the field driving a tractor that pulled a combine. My friend, Leo Aichlmayr (ak' el my er), was working the combine, when a fellow ran out into the field to announce that Leo had been drafted into the Army. We said our goodbyes, and I did not give too much thought to where he might be once I joined the Navy.

Well, there I was at the radio base in New Guinea, riding with a few of my buddies in a jeep down to the beach where the movies were shown. We came across three Army soldiers along the way. Oddly enough, one of them was Leo! I had not expected to meet up with anyone from St. Francis, Texas, halfway around the world, yet here he was. As pleased as I was to reconnect then, I found out that Leo had seen a great deal of time in battle. In one of those battles, he was one of only a handful of survivors. The war had affected his whole outlook on life. He had grown bitter. Leo felt he spent more time in harm's way than other soldiers. I wished him well when he was sent off by the Army on another assignment. I learned just a few weeks before our time to return home that Leo had been killed.

A short time after running into Leo, I received a letter from Amarillo saying that another friend, Maynard Bichsel (bik' sel), was on *The Roschambeau.* "What a coincidence," I thought, "that Maynard would be assigned to the very ship that brought me to Finchaven." Within days the ship arrived at our harbor. We had a small mail boat that would go out to retrieve letters and packages from ships that came from the States. So I hopped on that mail boat and went out to *The Roschambeau* and found Maynard.

They were anchored for a week or so, which gave us time to spend together. We decided a swim was in order. Although we usually swam in the buff, some nurses had come to the island and we were told to use swimming trunks. Now, coming from north Texas, my vast experience with swimming had been limited to that windmill water tank as a kid. We had very little practice with the ocean or with currents. In fact, Maynard could not swim at all.

We got caught in an undertow and Maynard had to hold on to my swim trunks for dear life. I swam with every ounce of my being only to be pulled back. I would make a bit of progress toward the shore only to be swept back out. I tried relentlessly over and over again. My strength was very nearly gone when I could barely feel the sand under my feet once more. We narrowly survived, and I am glad to report that Maynard returned to Amarillo after the war years, safe and sound. The outcome would have been quite different if I had not been wearing swim trunks that day.

How clearly I see that our lives are not just random little paths. During my nineteen months in the War, I had the opportunity to see folks from my tiny town in Texas, all the way out in the Pacific. I realize now just how much God is in control, all the time. He knows the exact moment we are going to enter into eternity, and likewise, He knows when our days are not done.

Beer Sick

Despite God's steadfast protection on the ship and in the ocean, I believe He let me suffer the consequences of my decisions, which were not always the wisest. After a year at Finchaven, the Navy provided us with a weekly allotment of beer. Now, I have always enjoyed a good cold beer and I looked forward to my own quart.

"No way, are we each using ours," said some of my Navy buddies. "We are going to pool the resources and draw for who gets it all that week. That gives us enough so we can get drunk." When my time came, I was on duty that evening and I drank two quarts before my shift and then begged the fellow in charge at the time to let me go get another. The beer we were given was stronger than what was usually served in the States. After three quarts of the stuff, I was so affected that two seamen took me back to my tent. I was sick for days. One man told the commander that I had not been to work in three days. The commander sent someone to get me.

He said, "I understand you have not reported for duty."

"Oh, no sir, I have been sick, so sick I have been vomiting."

He replied, "Yes, you look sick." Without further questioning, he called an ambulance right then and there and sent me to the hospital.

I sent word back to the guys not to explain the cause of my sickness. To my knowledge, the commanding officers never heard a thing.

Dear John

There were twenty-one men in our radio company, and before we left New Guinea all but two of us had received "Dear John" letters. These letters were from wives or girlfriends who had grown tired of waiting on their soldiers to return home. They were often harder to take than enemy fire. One fellow said he knew he would not be getting one, as he had been through a very long engagement and had already bought a home with his fiancée. Just shortly before our time to leave, he received his letter.

He was greatly depressed; we were honestly concerned that he might attempt suicide. There was a young fellow from New Orleans that came up with a plan to help. He asked each one of us for little photos of our sisters and girlfriends, and he composed a letter for our friend to send back to the fiancée along with all the girls' photos. It said, "Oh darling, I got your letter and I am just torn up about it, but for the life of me, I can't remember which one of these is you. Would you please take out your picture and send the others back?"

What Will the Future Hold?

I received a letter in New Guinea saying that the Army had drafted my brother, Arnold. It included a picture of him in uniform. Although he was still a kid when I left, somehow or other, he had grown up while I was away. He too was sent to the Pacific and served as his company's cook. He was involved in several battles, but I am very pleased to say that he survived the war. Arnold returned to the Amarillo area to be a farmer. I had a feeling he would do well as a man of the soil, but I did not know I would soon have a small part to play in his farming future.

As for me, I had several options. Early on, my superiors in the Navy asked if I wanted to attend

Officer Candidate School. Despite the leadership skills they saw in me, I wanted to stay with my Navy buddies who were fellow draftees and enlisted men. A long-term career at sea was a fine choice for other men, but my roots were in the soil. So I planned to return to Texas and farm next to my brother.

"You really ought to go to college when you leave the Navy," encouraged one of my officers. "Seriously, you should look into it. The G.I. bill will pay your tuition."

That got me investigating what colleges in Texas offered courses that would be beneficial to me. I found a program at Texas A&M University in Practical Agriculture. Although it was not a full-scale four year degree plan at the time, it sounded as though it would suit me, adding to my farm experiences and preparing me for a career in agriculture. I had no idea how God would direct my path, putting each little detail in place.

Out of the Navy

I returned to the States just before the war ended. I had a few months in Massachusetts and then went to New Orleans for my release. I attended a Catholic Church and went to a breakfast for service men where a woman asked what I would do next. I told her about my plans that included Texas A&M.

She replied, "But that's not a Catholic college! If you go, you be sure to join the Newman Club. It's for Catholic students at secular colleges."

Armed with the strong suggestion that I look up the Newman Club I applied to A&M and went home to St. Francis for a visit that turned out to be a timely event. Arnold had married and gone to work on one of the farms run by Joe Berg.

When I got home, we discovered that Mr. Berg was going to lease one of his farms, and since Arnold already worked for him, he was a good candidate. There was one major problem; to lease the land meant Arnold would need his own equipment, and he certainly did not have that kind of money. I had heard of a federal loan program to help folks working in agriculture. Just as I was on the phone speaking with a man about a loan, I saw Joe Berg drive by. The fellow on the phone helped me secure the financing for Arnold quickly, and I felt compelled to run after Joe. I just had a feeling he was on his way to lease the farm to someone else. I caught up with him and let him know that Arnold would soon have the money for the machinery. As it turns out, Joe had been on his way to finish the deal with someone else. In the nick of time, the Lord had intervened. Arnold took hold of that opportunity with both hands and farmed that land for many years.

A Namesake

One pleasant surprise after WWII was hearing from my radio school buddy and fellow Finchaven volunteer, Joe Thompson. He contacted me to say that his mother had another child just about the time Joe came home from the war. His mom had given Joe the task of naming the baby boy. To my delight, he decided to name the baby Herman. I had gained a namesake.

On to College

I was off to Texas A&M University and attended Mass my first Sunday. Afterwards, I remembered the advice of the lady in New Orleans and I asked about joining the Newman Club.

Father Valenta, the priest there, agreed that it would be a grand idea. "But oh gosh," he said, "I wish we had one!"

So I said, "Well then, let's organize one." That is exactly what we did and it influenced the rest of my life. I did not foresee what would become my next mission.

Chapter Four
The Newman Club, Washington, and Beyond

A MAN PLANS HIS COURSE,
BUT THE LORD DETERMINES HIS STEPS.
PROVERBS 16:9

The newly established Newman Club of Texas A&M University elected me President. Just a few months later, we received a letter from the chapter at the University of Texas in Austin announcing a regional meeting for Texas, Oklahoma and Arkansas. By the time that convention was over, I was President of the region as well.

Taking up a Cause

I did not know that one of my first tasks would come as a request from Prairie View A&M, a college for African American students just outside of Houston. They wished to establish their own Newman Club. Keep in mind this was 1945. When I brought this before the Board of Directors, we agreed that Prairie View should have a Newman

Club, but that it would not be any different from any other chapter on any campus.

We knew this might be a challenge, as students from one club were often invited to events hosted by other chapters. The Texas A&M campus did not allow a black person to enter unless that person was a campus employee. Although I had been raised to respect all people, that was not the norm then. The widely accepted view was that people of color were inferior. I never did believe that; I had no reason to. However, I did believe that I had a duty to help others, especially if they were asking for help.

We had arranged for the Newman Clubs of Texas, Oklahoma, and Arkansas to hold a convention at a nearby hotel. I contacted the hotel management the day before we were to begin. "Have I mentioned that we have delegates coming from Prairie View A&M?"

"Not in this hotel," was the reply.

"But we have to let them come, they are members."

"Not here."

So the night before the convention, I had to rush to find homes that would take us, including our six black students from Prairie View. Once we secured the lodging, we still did not have a plan for feeding us all. I went to the head of the chow hall at Texas A&M and told him what happened. "Could we possibly bring all of our delegates here?" I asked. I explained what "all" meant in this case.

"Well, this is probably going to mean my job," he said. "But, yes, bring them here."

We attended Mass the next morning and then headed to the chow hall, which was as noisy as ever. We interspersed the black students among us, but as the white students enjoying breakfast became aware of their presence, each voice grew still; you really could have heard a pin drop. Crashing the silence, one fellow jumped up and demanded in his long drawl, "Neusch, what the hell is goin' on here?"

I answered quickly, "Newman Club."

"Oh," he said and sat back down.

We served those delegates each meal at the Texas A&M chow hall without incident.

No Question of Loyalty

In these postwar years, the Catholic Church made a vocal stand against Communism as Russia extended her grasp into Eastern Europe. It was clear that our former ally was now a source of contention.

I became friends with the head of the YMCA near the college, and it surprised me more than a little when he called me in for an interesting report. "Last week," he said, "I got a call from the President of the University who told me that a student had qualified for a grant. Problem is, I hear he is a Communist." He asked me to check around and find out about this kid.

I did some looking and reported back to the President. "I don't know where you got your information, sir, but you are wrong. He is not a Communist at all."

"Well, I guess I should have told ya," said the President. "I did hear he was a member of that Newman Club."

That should have been all he needed to know. Catholics were most definitely not supporters of Communism. Our Church made this quite clear, and even as college students, we knew that Communism and its heavy-handed government would never be the answer to the world's problems.

A Shrinking World

That YMCA director at Texas A&M highly encouraged me to attend a new type of national convocation called "The Encampment for

Citizenship." He recommended me as one of 125 participants from all over the country that were selected to attend the six week long program in New York.

I think many adults in politics and industry in 1946 had grave concerns over the future of democracy and the whole role that youth would play in postwar America. There had been many youth service programs over the years, but this was really unique.

We lived together in a dormitory-type setting, girls in one section and boys in another. The "campers" really were a cross-section of the U.S. with youth from both rural communities and major cities. We represented different ethnic and educational backgrounds from both East and West. Some had just graduated from high school, some of us had served in the war, and most of us were in college. We came together each day for a great deal of discussion, guest lectures, and recreation. We covered just about every social issue you can imagine. Civil rights, economics, farm practices, religion, juvenile delinquency, political action, and labor laws were all topics for consideration.

This camp was quite an experience for me; I suppose I could call it life-shaping. For one thing,

I did not see myself as a natural leader, but others sure seemed to. We had elections during the camp to determine our own government. The gal who became President was friendly enough, but she did not know how to lead the group. When she resigned, I was asked to take the top position. I was willing to serve and began to see that I really could get people to work together.

The experience of our encampment, and others like it, is documented in a book titled *The Young Citizens* by Algernon Black. I am quoted in the book as "a farmer from Texas." Although some of the words attributed to me are not exactly accurate, it does rightly depict the purpose of the camp.

Helping Again

By this time, I had transferred from Texas A&M to the University of Texas at Austin. It seemed like a wise move for two reasons. First, I was moving into Economics instead of Agriculture and second, the Newman Club was well established there. Also, I would have easier access to State and church leaders in Austin. It was a hub of activity even in those days.

That move meant that I was in a position to know how effective our meetings had been. When the delegates to our A&M student convention had returned to their own campuses, the students at Prairie View spread the word about their positive experiences. Like many State colleges in those days, Prairie View A&M University offered weekly services on campus for Protestant students. Since there were only a few Catholics at that time, they had a priest come just every other Sunday for Mass. With all the publicity after our convention, one hundred students were soon attending Mass and asking for more services. Apparently this annoyed the college President. He made it a rule that any student who missed the campus-sanctioned service for two weeks would be expelled. He knew the impact this had on the Catholic students and would not relent from this position.

I got word of this and spoke with the priest at the UT Newman Club. We decided to take the issue to Governor Stevenson over at the Capitol. He listened to our concerns, made a call to Prairie View A&M, and that new policy was soon overturned. I was pleased to help them again.

Another opportunity to serve came my way in the summer of 1947. A second youth leadership conference was announced, this time to include international students. My experience with the Citizen Encampment had been so beneficial; I really wanted to participate in the second one. It was quite a privilege to be invited, as there were only eight delegates representing the U.S.A. The organizers of the camp sent us out to New Mexico so we would be isolated. That way, we could focus on each other and really listen.

I remember thinking what an amazing world we lived in during those post War years. The United States had championed democracy and I was becoming more aware of the political and spiritual influences that affected entire nations. During this leadership camp, I recall one young man from India who told us about the work of Mahatma Gandhi. I had heard of passive resistance that led to India's independence and to social reform, yet the first hand accounts from this student opened my eyes to the daily lives of citizens there. I felt great compassion for people around the globe and I felt a great pride in being an American. I loved serving in leadership.

The Bishops, the Banker, and the Passport
The time came for the national Newman Club convention, and I was elected vice president.

I also was elected vice president of Pax Romana, which literally means "Roman peace." That was the international arm of the Catholic Students Association.

One of the directors at the national convention announced there would be a meeting of Catholic students in Europe during that summer of 1948, and the U.S. wanted a representative present. None of us had plans to travel to Europe, so I asked him if I could get a letter stating I could serve as the U.S. delegate. He was quite enthusiastic.

My roommate at UT in those days was John Langley, and I showed him the letter when it arrived. I was a little skeptical about going all the way to Europe, knowing I would have to raise the funds, but John was insistent. "You mean if you had this letter, you would go?" I said.

"Heck yes," was his reply. He did not know it, but based on that response, I asked for another letter appointing him as a representative, too. John was quite shocked when his letter arrived. We were on our way to Europe; all we needed was the money.

One of our first efforts was to see two Bishops, one in Austin and one in Corpus Christi, Texas. Each of these church leaders wrote letters on our behalf, asking people to donate to our trip fund. Meanwhile,

I had another cause to work on that summer. The Texas A&M Newman Club was raising money to build a priests' home near the University. John went back to his hometown near Corpus Christi for the summer, along with instructions to get his passport ready for international travel and to raise money.

As our trip grew closer, I went to visit John and discovered he had not even applied for a passport! He thought it would be impossible to raise enough money in such a short time. I was not deterred, but with merely days to go, I knew we had to expedite it. Lyndon Johnson had just been elected to the Senate. I called him up and explained our predicament. He instructed us to "rush down to the U.S. Post Office and get a passport application sent by special delivery to Washington, D.C., and I'll help you get it done."

We went to Houston to raise funds and the Bishop had said we should call on a particular banker. So we called on the bank president and told him about our appointment to this international Catholic student conference and showed him the letter from the Bishop who had recommended we see him.

"Your Bishop sent you to *me*?"

"Oh, yeah."

He called in a few people to confer and then took us to a teller. "Write these fine gentlemen a check for five hundred dollars. Their Bishop recommended *me*."

"He is a Catholic, isn't he?" I asked the teller.

"Oh no," she replied. "He is one of the top Baptists in the city!"

Helped Along the Way

We needed every minute we had to raise more support. We had train reservations, but the train to D.C. would take too long, and we could fly for a only little more. So we traded in our train tickets and arranged to fly.

While we were calling on folks in Houston, we had heard of a well-to-do and charitable woman, Ima Hogg. Believe it or not, that really was her name, despite many stories to the contrary. I set off to find the high-rise apartment building where she lived. It had one of those phones in the lobby for calling the residents. She answered her phone and said she would come down to meet me. I presented our case and she wrote out a check right then and there.

"Let's see, you are representing all of the

Catholic students in Texas?" she asked when she was finished.

"Oh, no ma'am. In the whole United States."

"Really? Well, I should have given you more! If you don't raise enough, come back and see me and I'll give you more."

The day for our flight finally came. We had to pick up clothes at the dry cleaners and make one more appeal for funds. John was to hail a taxi, get the clothes, and meet me at the airport. I had a car and went back to see Miss Hogg, who was generous enough to complete the trip costs. By this time, I was running late to the airport. In fact, I was gunning down Main Street in Houston and nearly had a wreck. I stopped at a light and here came a taxi with the horn going and arms out the window, waving. I had passed up John on the way!

He grabbed the luggage, threw it in my car, and we were off to the airport. As we drove up close to the runway, I saw the stairs rolling away from the plane. I could see an open gate, and just as the plane started to taxi, I pulled right in through that gate and stopped the car in front of the plane. To say the least, the pilot sure wasn't very happy with me, but we got on that plane and made it to Washington.

The adventures continued in D.C. When

we arrived at the National Catholic Headquarters, John's passport was not there. We called the manager of the post office and explained to him our situation. It was Saturday evening and since our plane to Europe was departing on Sunday, we were desperate. The gentleman came down to the main post office and dug through many bags of mail with John until they found the right envelope. If I had not believed in miracles before, this would have been enough to convince me. Every detail for this trip came together, well beyond mere luck.

Europe at Last

John and I were so excited to set foot in Europe. As thrilling as it was to see the sights in Paris and Rome, we had a surprise during our tour of Vatican City. As we stood outside St. Peter's Basilica, we talked with a gentleman who asked our reason for traveling. We told him about the International Student Conference we were going to attend and how we were representing the U.S.

"Golly," he said, "you need to see the Pope while you are here." He disappeared for a few minutes and returned to say we should come back the next day. We were glad to do so. About ten tourists from all walks of life gathered the next day.

We were ushered into offices in St. Peter's where we met Pope Pius XII.

More Miracles

Just after that, we arrived in Geneva where the International Catholic student conference began. We kept hearing about the plight of displaced students, those who fled as Communism took over their respective countries. Many had sought shelter at a displaced student's camp in Hamburg, Germany. The more delegates spoke about them, the more intrigued I was. We had to go see for ourselves, but this was postwar Europe, and many eastern countries were closed to foreign travelers. It took special permission, if you were allowed to go at all. Geneva was the home of the League of Nations, so we went to officials there to ask for documentation allowing us to travel to Hamburg. Although I did not think of it as God's leading, I felt an urgent compulsion to go. John and I were determined to find the right channels and persist until we gained permission. The League of Nations granted us visas allowing us into Germany.

Meanwhile, we just happened to meet a man at the student conference who was from Frankfurt, who offered to help us enter Germany. Frankfurt was in great disrepair after the war, but we found a hotel that was held by the U.S. Army and asked to stay there. We showed our newly acquired visas, but the fellow at the hotel told us that our documents were only valid for German citizens. We weren't allowed to stay at the hotel. With some misgivings, the hotel staff allowed us to sleep in the lobby.

The next day, we met a priest named Father Paul McManus and told him about our desire to go to Hamburg to see the students in need and our dilemma with our paperwork. At the time, there was a shortage of everything, including transportation services. We had seen packed train cars coming and going from the city. I don't just mean crowded, I mean people were sitting up thick even on top of the cars.

However, Father McManus had a travel card that qualified him to get a ticket on a military train. It just so happened that John had served in Germany during the war and had a card showing he was military personnel. The only problem was that the card had been punched through with the letters V-O-I-D upon the end of his service there.

They stood in line anyway; Father McManus was first and asked for a ticket to Hamburg.

"Let us see your passport and your travel card."

He presented both and was issued a ticket in his name. John stood behind him and said, "I'm going with him."

"Passport and travel card?"

John showed his passport and then pulled the marked card up out of his pocket for just an instant and then quickly shoved it back down. It worked. He received a ticket for the military train and Father McManus gave his ticket to me.

Upon boarding, we discovered the accommodations were really first class; we had a private room with beds and all. Just before the train pulled away from the station, here came two military policemen checking each person's ticket and passport. I had to comply.

I handed over the passport with my name on it and the ticket with the name Reverend Paul McManus. The fellow took my passport, held it in his left hand and then placed the ticket right on top of it. He read over the ticket and then handed both documents back to me. I let out a long, slow sigh of relief.

I want you to know that the train stopped two more times before reaching Hamburg, and every time, the military policemen asked to see our passport and ticket. Each time, they followed the same routine, placing the ticket on top of the passport. No one noticed that my ticket and the name in my passport did not match! In addition, no one discovered that John's card had been clearly marked VOID. I have to consider that a miracle of divine protection.

A Difficult Plight, a Worthy Fight

We arrived in Hamburg to find a most amazing and distressing sight. Students had fled to Germany illegally from countries such as Poland and Czechoslovakia as Communism spread. They were refugees in every sense of the word, and quite literally, they were starving to death. Not a nation in the world would accept them. I am telling you, it was horrible. That kind of thing gets to your heart. Someone had to do something.

It just so happened that while John and I were still in Europe, the U.S. Congress passed the Displaced Persons Law of 1948. That allowed two hundred thousand "DP's" to come to the States, provided that they had suitable housing and employment without keeping a U.S. citizen from those privileges.

I heard about this law and about the oversight committee that President Truman had appointed. It was comprised of a Catholic man, a Jewish man, and a Protestant. I took that news to heart as John and I flew back to New York City and caught a train to Washington D.C.

We arrived about 10 p.m., and somehow or other, I had gotten the name of the Catholic man selected for the committee. I had the faces of those poor student refugees firmly in my mind as I called. I asked the appointee if study at a university could meet the requirement for "suitable employment" under the new Displaced Person Law. Of course, we would need to find housing for them.

"We are meeting tomorrow morning to decide the details," he said. "Can you come see me right now?"

It was after 10 p.m. and I had to get John out of bed, but this was too important to pass up. We met with the gentleman for a good hour or so. I made my argument that these students would be an asset to our campuses and simultaneously they would gain a good perspective on the United States. The appointee said he would make my recommendations to the Congressional Oversight Committee the next day.

He must have been effective because he called the next afternoon with the news: the Committee had decided to allow up to ten thousand of the two hundred thousand immigrants to be students. I took that information to heart.

I went to every kind of student meeting I could find to publicize the plight of these fellow students and promote this great opportunity to bring them to the U.S. I would hear of conferences at colleges in the Midwest or the Northeast and fly off to attend, whether I was a scheduled speaker or not. I talked to many students informally, and they would request that I speak to the whole convention. My specific plea was for the students to find housing for the DP's.

In those days, a fraternity or sorority house could squeeze in another student with practically no cost to those already living there. It was a legitimate solution, completely legal, and may I say, effective. I was aware of about five hundred foreign students who were able to gain housing in this way. I suspect that across the nation, there were many more.

While I was out promoting this cause, I received a call one day from the priest serving at UT's Newman Club who said I had to return to register for classes right away. The following day was the deadline for the semester! I came back to Austin just long enough to complete my registration and fly out again for another conference. I was filled with passion for this cause. It was my mission.

As it turned out, several immigrant students came to the University of Texas at Austin and became quite successful later in life. One of them was a Polish student named Anatol Falkowski. As I remember, he changed his name to Andy Falk and pursued a career in business. He became a vice president for Ralston Purina in South America. You can well imagine how significant his coming to the U.S. was. He was quite literally rescued from a dark future with little promise.

I know that I had some small part in bringing foreign students to the U.S. I also know who brought the details together. Imagine, poor Catholic kids from Texas making it on a plane to Washington and then getting a passport in the nick of time to fly to Europe. I do not doubt for one second that the Lord allowed John and me to travel to Hamburg to see those students. He knew my zeal for their cause would influence how Congressional law should be put into effect. It was a tremendous privilege and I must say, I felt truly blessed to have a part in this big plan.

Chapter Five
A Person of Influence

ENLARGE MY TERRITORY.
I CHRONICLES 4:10

Engaging

With the summer of '48 and the amazing experiences of Europe behind me, I looked forward to the fall semester at the University of Texas. I took every chance I could to tell the story of the displaced students and promote the Newman Club.

One day at Mass, an attractive young woman named Zita Kennedy caught my eye. When I would see her on campus, she always seemed to be in the company of another young man. I was quite relieved to find out that the other fellow was her brother.

"I first heard Herman speak at a campus theater for a rally. He talked about the student refugees," says Zita. "Even in those days, he was raising awareness and support for a good cause. Well, oddly enough, just after seeing him speak, I had the wild thought come to my mind that I would marry him. I never had such impulsive notions."

Zita had come to the university from the Texas Panhandle, as well. Her hometown was Pampa. While I came from a very large family, Zita's was small. Her brother was a UT student, and when her Dad passed away, she and her mother moved to Austin.

She tells the tale of preparing for our first date. She wanted to iron her sundress to make a fitting impression. We had talked about going to a movie, but when I arrived, I changed the plan and asked if she would like to go fishing first. She seemed a little surprised by this request.

"Yes, it was a surprise, but, when you know Herman, you know that fishing is his favorite thing to do, so he assumes everyone enjoys it. Besides, he was so handsome with his blond wavy hair and crystal blue eyes. He was just so -- overwhelming. He wore a white shirt every day and I was so impressed with the sleeves rolled up, you know. I did find out later that all he had to do was send them to the laundry because it was cheap in those days. But I was the one still ironing my dresses at home."

She consented to go fishing in her starched dress, so we set out to borrow a boat from a friend. Out on the water, Zita stood up in the boat and started to cast her line, only it had a lure with treble hooks. She had seen her dad fly fish where you cast the line out. I had to stop her real fast before she hooked one of us. Zita had a quick lesson on fishing with a hook. After that adventure, we did make it to the movies.

We would meet regularly at the Catholic Student Center for many functions, including dances. "That was a lot of fun and a good, safe place for students," Zita recalls "They didn't serve alcohol or anything, it was just about the dancing."

Pretty soon Zita told me she needed a tutor.

"Yes, I was struggling in Economics. I didn't understand a word the professor said. I made a D the first semester and had to do something. Well, Economics was Herman's major, so he tutored me, and the next semester, I made a B."

A Call to Serve

In the spring semester of 1949, I received a request from President Truman asking if I would come to Washington to serve on a committee overseeing "The Midcentury White House Conference on Children and Youth." The planning for the conference was already underway and would bring together the brightest thinkers and activists of the day related to American youth. This tremendous opportunity meant I would have to transfer schools. Before I left Texas in August of 1949, I asked Zita to marry me, and we began a long distance engagement.

"Oh, yes," she says. "I have quite a boxful of letters I received the whole time Herman was in Washington. I think they came every day, special delivery."

I arranged my classes at George Washington University in the mornings. At noon, I would dash over to the office of the National Catholic Welfare Council, or NCWC. I worked diligently, some days until midnight. I served as Vice President of the National Newman Club Federation.

Somehow I became the point man for a Holy Year trip in which two thousand Catholic young people would go to Rome in the summer of 1950. Every twenty-five years, the Catholic Church holds a special celebratory year in which many people make a pilgrimage to Rome. This was the first Holy Year since the end of WWII, and it was a focal point of hope for many Catholics. It was my job to register each participant and book their transportation and accommodations. With that many people traveling together, the trip plans alone meant I had to book three transatlantic ships and twenty-one planes.

The work was fascinating. The White House Conference would culminate near the end of 1950 with four days of meetings that would bring together six thousand delegates and represent over four hundred and fifty governmental and social agencies addressing the physical, emotional, and social needs of children and teens. The White House had hosted youth conferences each decade, but this one was the largest and would fall at the very middle point of the century. I had contact with a number of well known people on the committee such as Eleanor Roosevelt, Dr. William Mayo, and Dr. Benjamin Spock to name a few.

One of the impressive fellows was Walter Reuther, who came from negotiations with the auto industry. Although he had once supported socialism, Reuther had turned squarely to the U.S. Democratic Party where he campaigned for labor reform. He had insight on the growth of industry and our need for a prepared work force. It was a historic setting, and I knew the conference would influence our country for years to come. Despite my hard work in the planning, it turned out that my own life took a different course, and I would not be in Washington by the end of the year.

Taking a Toll

The pace of my life was crushing. I believed that I might not live past thirty-five if the demands on me continued at the same rate. I was responsible for many details in Washington and needed to maintain contact with Zita, who was planning a June first wedding in Pampa, Texas.

I was so busy, my grades slipped considerably. It was all I could do to work at the National Catholic Welfare Council and keep up with the White House Conference planning. I had students take notes for me in class, and I did my best to study when time allowed, yet I made all D's and one C. When I went to register for the spring semester, I was told I would have trouble graduating. I reminded the registrar that I had good grades with my transfer hours from Texas. She smiled.

"Well, you have to have good grades from here." It turns out she meant not just good, she meant all A's and one B.

The semester drew to a close. My wedding was near, and I had one incredible summer ahead. But I was leaving George Washington University one A short of graduation. It had come down to a one-question essay exam that I scored an 87 on. Despite my request to the professor for a rereading, my essay was not reconsidered, and for the sake of three points, I had not graduated. Life would not wait for that to be resolved.

A Texas Wedding and Two Thousand to Rome

"I remember our elegant rehearsal dinner at a country club," recalls Zita. "I looked down the row with everyone seated and noticed the parfait glasses. As people finished they would set their spoons aside, but not Herman. No, he wasn't concerned with etiquette; his spoon rested in his glass. Isn't that wonderful? He was not worried at all about being just like everyone else.

"I had come to realize that Herman was different. The way he was raised was certainly different than the way I was. His mother didn't bother to dust or keep house at all really. It was West Texas and the dust would blow through regularly. I was well acquainted with dust as my mother had made me dust our furniture every afternoon when I came home from school. But not Herman's mother; their house was a mess. Yet he never once apologized for her. I think his ego was not in the way."

As with most weddings, there was a difficult detail that had to be overcome. My luggage was lost en route from Washington to Pampa and I had to run quickly to rent a tux. Of course, that nearly made me late for the wedding. However, the moment arrived, and we were married on a Thursday morning at Holy Souls Catholic Church and then took off on a honeymoon with two thousand people, including my mother-in-law!

Well, that is not totally true. Zita and I had a brief side trip, just the two of us to New Mexico, but we had to return quickly because we were going with the Catholic students on the Holy Year trip.

For Zita and me, the Europe trip soon grew to become a global one. On our previous trip, John and I had contact with a democratic youth organization called the World Assembly of Youth, or WAY. I was asked to represent them around the world. That meant Zita and I would continue traveling to several cities, while the President of the Newman Club Federation would take over the Rome trip. Our paperwork was in place, and we were scheduled for a series of student conferences that would take six months to complete.

"There were many firsts on the trip," Zita recalls. "We flew to New York City to connect with an Italian ship. We had gone into a restaurant with a long buffet, and at the end was this little box with black and white pictures. Imagine, our first look at television! It was quite something. Anyway, it was on the ship that they served us a dish made from flatbread and tomato sauce. It was a new treat we had never tasted before. Pizza!"

We sailed across the Atlantic, enjoyed some beautiful sunsets, and made our way to France. We met up with some very dear friends of ours, Don and Ruth Sullivan, in Paris.

"We attended Mass each morning," Zita says. "Because there were so many cathedrals in Europe, you could pick a different one each day. But we did have a favorite, a small one in Paris, that we went back to."

While Zita had a chance to tour Paris for a few days, I attended a symposium in Brussels sponsored by WAY. Then, we were off to Switzerland to visit the world headquarters of Pax Romana. As if the sights were not coming quickly enough, we had a few days in Venice, Italy, where we were enchanted by the canals and the gondolas.

However, very little can compare with Rome. St. Peter's Basilica is the largest Catholic Church in the world and there really is no way we could prepare ourselves for all its majesty. We saw world-class paintings and sculptures at the Vatican Museum and Art Gallery. We took in famous stops such as the

Coliseum, the Sistine Chapel, and the Catacombs. Each one is breathtaking in its own way. Yet before long, it was time for Zita and me to leave our group behind and make our way east.

On to India

Our journey took us to East Pakistan where I had a cousin serving as a priest. After a few days visit, we traveled to several cities in India, including Bombay. The contrast to the cities we had seen in Europe was compelling. Despite the ruins left from bombings during WWII, countries in Europe were much more modernized. It was clear that industrialization had barely begun in India by 1950. Life was much slower there. All the work was done by manual labor and ox cart. We viewed a dam that had taken over twenty years to build.

My appointment with WAY meant I was one of a few internationals given an opportunity to meet Prime Minister Nehru who had come to power after Gandhi. He brought us to his home for an entire day where we met his daughter as well. She became a political leader in India years later. This meeting turned out to be the start of ongoing correspondence. I worked to set up a student exchange program that brought college students to the U.S. from India. It was evident that the youth of the country had no knowledge of life in the West, and one good way to affect their thinking was to bring students over to live and study on U.S. campuses. After our success with the Displaced Persons Act, I was hopeful. Yet I was not able to see it through.

TB

At another student conference in India, we came across a mobile unit that took chest X-rays to determine if people had TB. Tuberculosis was quite a concern in the 1950's, so I decided to stop by. My X-ray showed that I was infected. It was not unusual for hotels to have a doctor, so I checked in with him. He gave me shots of streptomycin, which was very new at the time. The drug was considered effective against TB, but was in no way a complete cure. In addition, it had an unpleasant side effect on hearing. To this day, I have ringing in my ears.

I took a side trip to Sri Lanka, the big island off the coast of India. In those days, it was called Ceylon. Zita remained in Calcutta while I was there. I came down with a travel bug that was bad enough that the hotel called in a doctor. When he listened to my chest I asked, "Hear anything funny?"

"No, should I?"

"I've been told I have TB."

Well, that happened to be his specialty, and he took me to his clinic that was outfitted with equipment that could show my breathing in motion, rather than a still shot like an X-ray. He said that I did have the disease and my prognosis was so serious that I needed to return to the U.S. immediately. So I returned to India to meet up with Zita and we began our journey home.

International flights were less frequent in those days, and you couldn't just hop on a plane any time you wished. We joined the Sullivans again in Paris and tried to get all four of us on a transatlantic flight. There was only room for two. The doctors said my condition was so grave that I could die within days, so the decision was made that Don would accompany me on the first available flight back to the U.S. because he had contacts at a clinic on the east coast that I could enter immediately. Zita and Ruth followed a few days later. I was transferred to the Veterans Hospital in Temple, Texas, where I remained for six months.

Other Troubles

While I was required to be still in my bed at the VA Hospital, I decided to resolve my graduation issues with George Washington University. I wrote to ask if I could finish my studies by extension. They wrote back that they did not offer that option and suggested I ask the University of Texas. Unfortunately, UT required I attend class in person the last semester before graduation.

I tried again, making an appeal to the President of my college in Washington. I told him my whole story. He denied my request, but said I could write a letter that would be sent to all of the Deans, and if they approved, I could be awarded a diploma. They rejected my letter, but said I could write another appeal to be sent out to each professor. By this time, my tone was more confrontational. The last thing I got from George Washington University was a bill for thirty-five dollars for the printing of my diploma.

Our first child was born in March of 1951, and against the VA's recommendation, I left the hospital. In those days the principal "cure" for TB was total rest. I did not get out of bed to make trips to the bathroom without the help of a nurse and a wheelchair. I suppose it was effective enough, but six months was all I could take. Besides, I needed to be with Zita and the addition to our little family.

So with my returning health, a diploma in hand, and a young wife and infant, we moved back to Washington D.C. It was a hard time for me. I think my influence there had waned, and I didn't seem to be in the flow of things. However, I was asked to attend a youth organization meeting in Africa. About eight to ten American students were selected to attend the conference in Dakar, a port city in Senegal, which in those days was called French West Africa. I distinctly remember Zita making me promise not to go lion hunting, and I held to that promise.

I also had one more opportunity to visit Paris as a U.S. delegate to the United Nations Educational, Scientific, and Cultural Organization, UNESCO. There were only two of us representing the U.S., so I counted it a privilege to be one of those chosen. I did not realize what I was in for. The Russians had opted out of UNESCO during the war years, and this was their first time to return with a delegation. And what a vocal group they were. It took us three days to elect a chairman, as the Russians would come to the podium and speak at length against the United States. They had quite a bit to say against their WWII ally. It made for a tense and long conference.

Back in Washington, we had a second child. Richard entered the world and was quickly termed a colicky baby. I would pace up and down at night with him; he was restless and so was I. My time in D.C. seemed fraught with obstacles. I knew something had to change. I decided it was time to move out of the government arena and back to Texas. I just wasn't sure what job would await me.

Attempts and Offers

The return to Austin brought an offer to work in the oil and gas leasing business. Our third child, Esta, came quickly on the heels of the first two. So when the business offer required a good deal of travel, I turned it down. Yet with three tiny children and a wife to support, I had to come up with something. I discovered that the owner of Austin Electroplating Company wanted to sell his business. I borrowed money from folks in Amarillo and bought it. After a year or so, I was not successful and had to close the operation. That led me to a trucking company that asked me to sell on commission, but that did not work out well either.

I had met Jack Brown, the owner of a dry cleaning company in Austin, through a Catholic couples' club. I had the idea to go door to door and build his customer base by asking to clean one garment for free. So I asked Jack how many customers he could take.

"All you can get," he said. He paid me a small amount for each customer I brought in. Soon his statement proved untrue. "Herman, I can't handle any more business!" he told me before long.

The plan worked so well, I went to San Antonio and got three more dry cleaners there to do the same. The plan worked there, too, but that was a short-lived business deal. Soon I was ready to try a new adventure. I had heard about American General Life Insurance Company in Austin. It was a growing business, and that was good because I had quite a family to support.

"Yes, we certainly did," Zita agrees. "I married when I was just twenty-one years old and by twenty-five, I had a baby and a one, two, and three year old. I really think I might have been institutionalized had it not been for Herman's positive attitude. He would come home and find me in tears. He would help with the children and just come up with things that weren't really common then. He built a table just the right height for the children so they could play. You see, I was a bit of a perfectionist and the problem with perfectionism is that it just doesn't go with having four tiny kids!

"His perspective was just different. I knew Herman had grown up with seven siblings and was used to having many people in the house, but I did not realize how much small things meant to him. One time, when I was very tired and he was helping me fold the laundry, he teared up and said, 'Thank you, for these clean clothes.' I had seen washing and folding clothes as a tedious chore, but at that moment, I realized that he did not have clean clothes often as a child, and now he was grateful that he and his children had them."

Zita was right. I was grateful for many things in those days, including our brood of small children. I knew we needed coping strategies as parents. We found a bridge club comprised of other couples with large families and really enjoyed their company. I looked for creative ways for our kids to play and be engaged with each other. When they were a bit older I made stilts for each of our kids. It was great fun watching our children attempt to master this new form of transportation. Of course, I wanted them to have many life experiences, which had to include learning to hunt and fish.

From a Child's View

"Oh, yes, Dad always took us hunting and fishing, even the girls," says Esta. "I remember sitting in deer blinds in the freezing cold, trying to hold still and be quiet. It was a challenge, but it was so exciting. Dad would let us touch the deer after we brought them home. I always loved dissecting in high school science class. I wonder if that came from seeing the insides of all those deer.

"For some reason, I also remember Dad bathing the four of us big kids," Esta reports. "He'd put all four of us in the same tub and play games with us while we soaked clean. He gave us all bathtub names. I was *La Cucaracha*, which I thought was quite elegant until I found out it meant cockroach!"

"I wasn't more than four or five years old when I remember Dad taking me fishing," Richard recalls. "I had a Zebco rod and reel with a push button. You would hold the button in and then when you cast the line, you let the button out and the line would go out. I practiced casting and really had it down. I was so happy and wanted to show Dad, but when I let go of the button, I let go of the whole thing. The rod went sailing through the air. Dad was not deterred, though. He tied a rope around my waist and the pole in case I did it again. That way we could retrieve the rod.

"Now I had to wait until I was seven years old to shoot my first deer," continues Richard. "We had a 30/30 rifle, which is a really big gun with a lot of kick to it. Dad would not let me shoot it for fun; I had to wait until we were on a hunt. He had cut the stock in half because I was so small. He set me up in a tree and ventured off, maybe 200 yards away. Not too long after that a doe and fawn walked right out near me. I didn't know what to call them but Big Deer and Little Deer. I shot the bigger one and the small one skittered off, but came back hesitating. The little one lingered. I called out in the quiet, 'Dad?'

'Yes, son,' his voice came from a distance.

'I got one.'

'Ok. I will be there.'

'Dad?'

'Yes, son?'

'There's another one. It's a little deer. Can I shoot it, too?'

'No!'

That was the start of my years as a hunter."

"Then there was the time Dad took us all fishing," adds Esta. "A tornado came up over the horizon and scared us all. I didn't see anything else after that because I was on the floor of our station wagon praying! As the fiercest winds hit, our car swept sideways across the street. We were all okay, but that is one thing I'll never forget."

"As we got older, our family always had a boat or a lake house or property for camping. We went boating as a family and Dad taught us all how to water-ski. Dad would buy a boat in the spring, we would use it all summer, and then every fall he would sell it for more than he paid for it."

It's true, I did buy and sell boats for the family. We enjoyed the water, so I made a wooden plank that we pulled behind the boat. I had no idea then that some day you could buy a "wake board" for that purpose. You could say our kids had one of the very first ones.

I did my best to see that our kids had a full and rich life. With six children, I needed to make a good living, so I set out to do that by becoming a life insurance salesman. American General Life Insurance Company sounded like just the opportunity I needed.

Chapter Six
The House Payment

I approached forty friends and contacts about buying American General life insurance, and I did not sell a thing. Salesmanship is an art, but one that must be learned. Most agency managers trained their newly hired employees themselves and sent them to "new man school." Our manager was so busy, he did not have the time to train me, and I had not sold enough insurance to qualify for "new man school." He made an exception and sent me to a training session in Houston.

I met a fellow there who, despite his less than charming personality, had sold quite a bit of insurance in the Waco area. I called up his manager and asked if he could train me. He agreed and I traveled to Waco several times and learned well. In fact, I became the first person in the Austin area to sell a million dollars of life insurance in a year. I invited several of my friends to become part of the

Board of Directors of the 'Neusch Corporation for the Million Dollar Round Table' and they helped me reach that goal.

A Family House

By the early 1960's, our family had grown to six children and we needed a bigger house. In those days, the Burnet Road area was far North Austin, and we had an opportunity to build in a neighborhood right across from a school not far from Northwest Park. We had a friend that was an architect who drew up plans for a beautiful, spacious two-story home. I was pretty sure we could not afford to build such a place, but he suggested we solicit some bids. It turned out we could build our house for a price I could afford.

Zita says the house was a tremendous blessing since she was involved in about twelve car pools at the time. It brought her closer to many of those destinations. The home was built on Pineleaf Place, which was the northernmost street in the city. She could look out our windows on one side and see fields of Texas bluebonnets. Yet, we were not far from St. Louis Catholic Church, and Northwest Park boasted a swimming pool that our kids could walk to and swim in for one dime apiece.

Bill, our youngest son, liked to wander out in the undeveloped meadow. One day he went out with the dogs and came home with a report on his foraging for rabbits. "I saw millions and millions of 'em. At least four or five!"

Needing More

Despite my successes as an insurance man, I was aware of a growing need for more of something in my life. I was searching for something deep, genuine and satisfying. The Catholic Diocese of Austin offered a Cursillo, or "short course" consisting of a three-day weekend retreat, similar to the Protestant program called Walk to Emmaus. It included teachings from church leaders about the Christian faith, but also gave us time to be alone to hear from God ourselves. It sounded like just what I was looking for so I signed up.

In all my years in the Catholic Church, I had not been instructed on praying to invite Jesus into my heart, but that turned out to be just what I did. It wasn't fancy, but I knew I was in His presence and I knew that I wanted Him to use me. I prayed, "Lord, You use manure to fertilize roses, so please take my life now and do what you will with it." I believe that Jesus came into my heart and I had the Biblical experience of spiritual birth or being "born again." I grew steadily in my faith. I consumed books and attended all manner of teachings.

I also had a budding interest in real estate and began to buy small tracts of land at this time. My first purchase came through the Veterans Land Program and consisted of fifty acres with Lake Travis frontage for $150 an acre. That led me to more investments. I would keep a property for just two years and sell it for double the price I had paid.

God Speaks

I soon learned about the cloistered Catholic sisters in Austin who were committed to praying twenty-four hours a day in one hour shifts. There were not enough of them to cover the entire week, so men who had been to the Cursillo offered to fill in the time slots on Monday nights. My hour was from two to three in the morning. I think it was my very first time there that I did all the praying I could think of in my hour, but when three o' clock came, the man who was supposed to follow me did not show up. I sat down and waited. While I was sitting, not saying a thing, I had these words come into my mind:

"Go see Teeter about buying some land."

I heard God speaking to me! I wasn't speaking, He was.

Glen Teeter was a hunting and fishing buddy of mine. We had been on several trips together, but I had no idea Teeter was about to buy real estate. I was so excited that I could not sleep the rest of the night. I called him very early Tuesday and asked him out to breakfast. "Are you trying to buy land?" I asked.

"I sure am."

"Where?"

"Out in Oak Hill."

"How much land do they have?"

"Something over a hundred acres. They agreed to sell me twenty acres, but won't sell the rest."

"Let's go look at it."

We drove by the property, and on the gate was a sign that read, "Not for Sale. Good-bye. Thank you."

We drove back to Austin, but I was determined to follow through. I asked Teeter to let the people know I wanted to buy their land. Meanwhile, I planned to stop by a bank to borrow money. It was still the Tuesday morning after the Monday night of prayer, but it couldn't wait.

I went right over to see a banker. I was quite excited about the idea of buying land. This land. After all, The Lord had spoken to me and I wanted to obey. I insisted that the banker come with me to Oak Hill at that moment. He objected, but I persisted, and we went for a drive. I told him my intention to buy that very property, despite the sign, and that I needed thirty thousand dollars to do it.

He said, "Herman, it is not legal for me to lend you money to buy raw land."

"Alright, lend me thirty thousand dollars. I will buy that land and put it up as security for the note."

"Oh, I can do that."

Next I contacted Teeter, who reported rather excitedly that the owners wanted to meet with me.

A House Payment

The owners were the Thurmans, a couple approaching ninety years old who were devout Christian believers. We must have talked for an hour or so, and they agreed to a sale price of thirty thousand dollars. However, they did not want the payment all in cash. They asked me to find them a home near their church in Austin. "Buy us a home and give the difference in cash," they said. I asked several realtors to help me locate a home, but no one called me.

One day, Teeter and I were driving about a block from their church when we passed a home with a one by four piece of lumber nailed up in a tree. There was not a word on it; it had been there so long. "Stop here Teeter," I said. "That might have said 'For Sale' at one time."

I knocked on the door. "Sir, do you want to sell your house?"

"I sure do."

"What are you asking for it?"

"Twelve thousand dollars."

It was a nice little house with a garden in the back. I took the Thurmans to see it. They loved it. I proceeded with the loan and helped them move in. Mrs. Thurman told me that she had not really wanted to sell her home in the country, but she needed to move in town; they were totally dependent on others to transport them. The Sunday before I had arrived, her pastor had asked for folks to stand who were in need of prayer.

"Well, I stood up, but the Lord immediately said to me, 'Sit down, Novela, I am taking care of it.' Then, two days later, on Tuesday morning, you came out to buy our land."

The Rest of the Story

I named the hundred-acre development Mountain Shadows. I hired a contractor and a surveyor to plot five-acre tracts and went to the County to get approval for the subdivision. The roads and utilities were put in place, and the properties sold in short order. I was becoming a successful real estate developer, with quite an insurance business as well.

Rolling Oaks

My excitement over this venture was barely containable. I really wanted to pursue another land deal. As intense as my longing was, I knew to pray before I did anything else. The desire to buy land was matched with an equally intense yearning to know God and pursue His ways. The two seemed intertwined. I attended a men's prayer breakfast and shared with them my passion for real estate. One gentleman said, "If you have that desire, the Lord put it there."

That was all I needed to hear. That very day I called a realtor and told him what I wanted to do. It turned out that he knew of 1,100 acres in Hays County, near Kyle. My friend Buck Daily had said that the next time I bought property, he wanted in on the deal. So Buck and I went as partners to meet the owner.

An attorney held the deed to the land. He was one shrewd fellow; dealing with him was like sitting in front of a rattlesnake. He wanted over two hundred dollars per acre with financing that we could not begin to afford. Buck and I conferred privately. Buck was ready to run out of there, but we told the attorney we would have to go see our financial backer. Of course, we didn't have one yet.

I went straight to the Catholic Chancellery office to speak to their investment director about borrowing from the Bishop. It just so happened they were interested in seeing the property and adding to their holdings. Every one of the details came together, and we were able to buy the land. We named it Rolling Oaks Ranch. My vision to buy and sell land had become a reality.

How Odd of God

Despite the excitement I felt over real estate sales, my soul was stirring. I wanted to be close to God, to know Him with every fiber of my being. That intense desire led me to certain books and to certain people. I read *Prison to Praise* by Merlin Carothers and *Nine O'clock in the Morning* by

Dennis Bennett. These books intrigued me with their stories of the Holy Spirit and His effect on people's lives.

I heard about a movement of God at a ministry near the UT campus called The Well. I went there and prayed to receive the baptism of the Holy Spirit. This experience was not unique to me at this time; Catholics and Protestants all over the Austin area were touched in the same way.

In fact, my friend Father Underwood at Dolores Catholic Church was experiencing much the same thing. Father Fred had arrived in the Montopolis area of Austin in the early 1960's. He had seen the poverty, poor housing, and delinquent kids. He worked diligently to change all of that. He helped build a Community Center and campaigned for better bus service, as most of the people in the area did not own cars and needed transportation to stay employed. This simple action on his part had a huge impact on many families. Within a few years, the crime rate had dropped and decent homes replaced the substandard housing.

I had the privilege of speaking on Pentecost Sunday to the congregation, along with two other laymen. We took this chance to tell others about our friendship with Christ. After the service, many people stayed for prayer, experienced God's presence, and received the baptism of the Holy Spirit.

The Church was transformed. A great desire for God swept over us and through us. One result of our speaking on Sunday was the start of prayer services on Wednesday nights in English and in Spanish. I mean deep, passionate prayer. With standing room only, entire crowds saw many miracles, including people healed of diseases and long-term conditions.

I know these events might sound odd, but I want you to know that something supernatural yet very real was happening. There is no logical explanation for miracles. God did them and the people received great benefits. This prompted even more desire in our hearts to seek the Lord.

No Scales

About this time, I had the great privilege of speaking about my faith to several groups. One invitation came from the women at St. Ignatius Catholic Church in South Austin. As I spoke, something came out of me that I had not intended to say.

I told them that as a Catholic, I used to think that God sat up in heaven with a big set of scales. If I did something good, he put a weight on one side. If I did something bad, he put a weight on the other side. I would just have to be sure by the end of my days that I had more weight on the good side. That way, I could make it into Purgatory at least when I died.

I had come to realize how foolish and wrong this line of thinking is. Clearly, if I could put enough weight on the good side, there would be no reason for Christ to die on the cross. It takes the most amazing gift, God's mercy and righteousness, and says back to Him, "We don't really need this."

"That is a damnable theology!" I shouted. I had not intended to be so loud, but there I was, shouting. Just then, I spotted the priest sitting at the back. He was nodding his head. Apparently my old view was not accurate or God-honoring, and my new understanding had resonated with the priest.

The Challenge and Increasing Faith

It was an amazing time for me, yet the more I knew of God and pursued Him, the more Zita and I grew apart. She was on her own journey. While I could not get enough of Christ, she was moving into Eastern thought. Somewhere along the way, she stopped attending Mass. This was an enormous obstacle that I did not know how to overcome. I pressed on with two clear missions that I could pursue: business endeavors and my growing faith.

While I attended Dolores Catholic Church, I was invited to a Full Gospel Businessmen's meeting. As I entered, one gentleman watched me from across the room. He kept his eye on me throughout the meeting and then approached me with these words:

"God will greatly increase your faith."

He said he sensed this message from the minute I walked in. Immediately after that I made two trips: one to see my uncle in Houston, and the other, a business trip to Dallas. While I traveled, I remembered what the fellow had said.

A Foundational Book

My uncle bought me a book by Mel Tari called *Like a Mighty Wind*. It tells about a church in Indonesia and how miracles occurred there as the villagers cried out to God. At one point, local people ran for water as they saw flames over the church building. Those inside were not burned by physical fire, but were set ablaze in their faith. Many were healed of physical ailments. The account is given of believers walking on water to cross a river as part of an evangelism effort.

The book became very important to me in my understanding of God's amazing power. It shapes me to this day. Some time later, I heard that Mel Tari would be in Texas. He stayed in my home for three days and we spoke together in a few churches.

Dallas Trip

When I traveled to Dallas after visiting my uncle, I stayed with a family while on business and met three very unique people. The first was a pastor. Instead of telling me his "life story," he told me his death story. He had literally been raised from death. As fantastic and unbelievable as that may sound, he knew it to be true and I had no reason to doubt his own account.

Then, I met a man who had his leg cut off at the hip by a small plane propeller. He was rushed to the hospital, and while the doctors looked over him, his leg was restored. He is a medical miracle.

If that were not enough, the lady of the house where I was staying told me about a crisis while she was pregnant. She began hemorrhaging and knew she and her baby were in grave danger. She, too, was rushed to the hospital. While unconscious, she tells of being able to see herself in the emergency room, as if she were watching from the ceiling. The doctors assumed her baby could not have survived such trauma. They removed the baby's body and set it aside, turning all their attention to saving the mother. At some point, the hospital was required to assess the baby only to find that she was still alive. The woman and her infant both survived.

To say the least, the man that watched me at the meeting had been quite accurate; God was greatly increasing my faith. I came to believe that He can do anything, from the highly unlikely to the down right impossible.

My stay was prolonged and I moved into a hotel. When I was finally preparing to leave Dallas, I had an unsettling sense that I should stay a little longer. I held my Bible and asked the Lord to guide me on whether to stay or go home. I let the Bible fall open and my eyes fell on Luke 24:49 which says, "I am going to send you what my Father has promised; but stay in the city until you have been clothed with power from on high." There was my answer. I knew it was meant for me, so I remained in Dallas.

While I was there, I attended an Episcopal Church service. There I came across a book that explained how to deal with spiritually dark forces. I found it revealing. I wanted to use these new tools, not realizing that I would have the opportunity to do so soon.

Using the Tools

I returned to Austin and found that a few families connected to Dolores Church had serious needs, and I could employ what I learned on my trips. It is a sobering thing to come against dark spiritual forces, but I had been prepared. Just as the man had said, God had greatly increased my faith. I could see His hand in the path I had taken, the people I had met, and the books I had read. God prepared me to pray with great faith and authority. As a result, the people were released from negative influences.

There is an unseen realm where good and bad forces are at work, but the power of Christ is greater than all of them. At times we see the effect of these forces on people through their physical bodies or upon their mental state. The fact that those forces are not visible to our eyes in no way means they do not exist. I was humbled by God's mighty power over darkness and that He chose to use me to help others in this way.

Camps Farthest Out

About this time, Father Underwood suggested it was time for me to consider full time ministry. I pondered this option. I reflected on my spiritual growth, my success in the insurance and real estate businesses, and also on my troubles at home. I was discouraged about my marriage. I needed to hear from God about this pressing problem, so I went to a retreat center called Camps Farthest Out.

While there, I walked out among the trees and poured out my heart to the Lord. I asked Him what purpose He had for me. Quite distinctly I heard, although not in an audible voice, "Herman, my purpose for you is to love Zita." At that point I realized how much I had been considering divorce. I had six wonderful children and a deep respect for the Church that does not condone divorce.

At that moment, I was flooded with love for her. Truly this was beyond human sentiment and emotionalism. Once again I had a mission. Often we may think that being assigned a mission from God will take us far away to exciting places, but sometimes our mission is much closer than we think. I did not have to travel far to obey this call. My mission was under my own roof.

I returned home with a renewed love for my wife. I felt something different towards her. I knew Zita and I had a long history together. I also knew that her spiritual path and mine had diverged and we were heading in very different directions. Yet, I had received love from God for her. I left the camp filled with love, and it sustained my marriage for twenty-five more years.

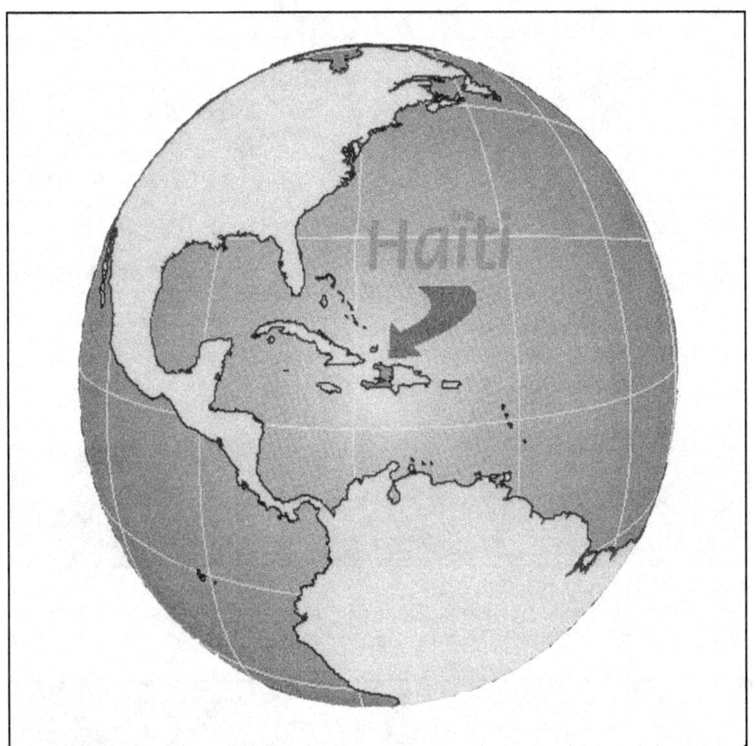

Herman's family: from left to right
Zona, Mom (Mary), Betty, Herman, Rosemary, Myrtle, Arnold, Dad (Bill). Not pictured is little brother Ralph, who died at 17 years old.

Herman enjoying his favorite pastime with little son Richard.

Herman as a teenager, portrait of
the young seaman.

The Navy buddies enjoy a meal. Joe Thompson is first on the
left, Herman is second from the right.

Herman, second from right, with fellow seamen in New Guinea.

Herman at the Coliseum in Rome.

Herman and John during their Vatican visit.

Herman stands behind President Truman with members of the National Newman Club.

Herman married Zita in the summer of 1950.

Then and now. Herman's first four children from left to right: Gay, Esta, Richard and Donna.

The six adult Neusch children: Donna, Richard, Esta, Mary, Gay and Bill.

Bill walks with Herman in Hungary.

Typical homes in Haiti.

A Haitian Mom and her children. Forty percent of Haiti's population is under 15 years old.

A crowded "tap- tap," a common means of transportation.

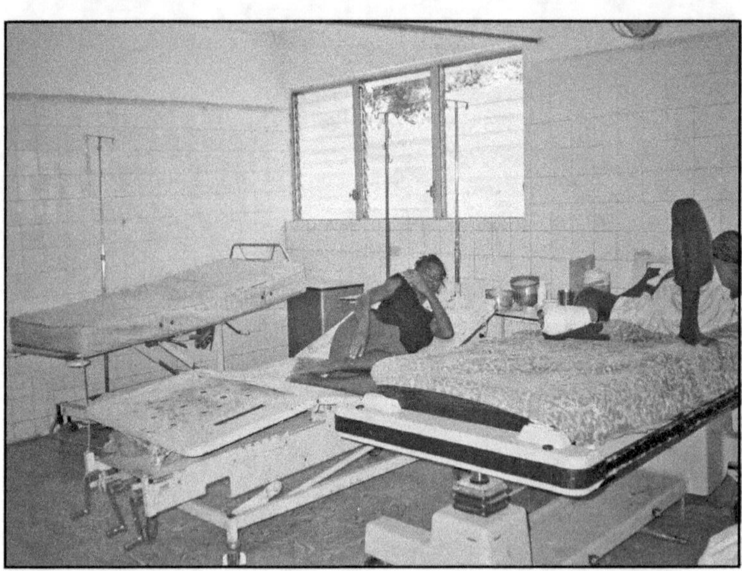

The hospital in Cap-Haitien, the second largest city in the country, is poorly supplied. Patients must bring their own medicines and sheets.

Flood waters inundated Haiti in 2008 when four hurricanes made landfall.

In addition to poverty and disease, Haiti faces severe water and transportation troubles in the aftermath of storms.

Workers turn the charcoal which is sold as cooking fuel. This practice has deforested most of Haiti.

A real solution, solar cookers arrive in Port-au-Prince.

Food for the hungry. Many vegetables such as cabbages and carrots grow well in Haiti when water is available.

Children walk long distances to collect water for their families. New and repaired wells provide this essential commodity that makes the gardens possible.

Herman and Janet with Christian school children on the island's north side.

A crowded pew during a visit to a church and school.

Education is in short supply. Here adults attend Bible School.

These smaller students are provided a Christian elementary education.

Herman meets a former voodoo priest who is now committed to following Christ.

Young and old. Herman meets a baby who is also named Herman.

Rubber bands are a simple treat and a fun treasure for the children.

Herman stands with Dennis and Jennifer Maupin, who are moving to Haiti. Bill Neusch (Hope for Haiti) and Randy Shipman (pastor, First Baptist Church, Clinton, Mo.) welcome these new partners.

A tractor tills the soil, preparing for another garden.

This New Holland tractor and rig will bring new water wells to a dry land and help establish new gardens.

Brimming baskets showcase a rich harvest.

Growing their own food brings satisfaction, dignity and hope to the people of Haiti.

Herman with granddaughter Elizabeth on a mission trip to Hungary in 2000.

Herman with the love of his life, Janet.

Chapter Seven
Majesty and Provision

AH, SOVEREIGN LORD, YOU HAVE MADE
THE HEAVENS AND THE EARTH.
JEREMIAH 32:17

By the 1970's, you could say I had three missions. I was soaking up all I could in my walk with God, I purposed to love my wife, and I had a passion for buying and selling land. I did not predict that these missions might some day collide. What I knew was that the five-acre tracts at Rolling Oaks Ranch were selling and that I could see God's hand in all manner of details. In fact, the real estate development business was going so well, I turned over my life insurance clients to another agent so that I could fully pursue my passion.

Renting a Bus

Sometimes the smallest things speak loudly. If you are willing to look, you can see the hand of God in them. That was certainly true in what I could call "the bus incident." I heard about a huge multi-denominational rally to be held in a football stadium in St Louis, Missouri. I really wanted to go and felt the Lord prompting me to rent a bus to take many people from Austin. As the time drew closer, it appeared that I had been wrong; with just days to go, very few people had taken my offer. I tried to talk folks into going. Nothing worked. It looked like my plan would be a total failure.

Then, I met a pastor who said he had many people in his church who would want to go, but had no arrangements on short notice. I told him I had a bus. It turned out that the number of people from his church exactly matched the number of seats on the bus. I had also made motel arrangements for a certain number of attendees. When we arrived, the number of rooms divided perfectly into the number of men and women on our bus. You can plan for exact numbers and not have it work this well. Although it may seem a small thing, I saw Providence in these precise, little details.

"I Found It"

I have seen God's hand in large events as well. While I attended Dolores Catholic Church, a Protestant group had a national campaign called "I Found It" to teach people how to lead others to accept the gift of Jesus as Savior. Although this was not a common practice among Catholics, we signed up and held training for several sessions. Now that was pretty radical stuff in 1973. Protestants and Catholics were not often found together. But here we were, Catholics, preparing to go door to door to share our faith.

Once the people of Dolores were prepared and had prayed considerably, we set out in pairs to canvas all of the area around the church. On a Saturday morning, we knocked on doors and spoke directly to people about our faith and asked if they would like to receive Christ. It is not an easy thing to do, but we had tremendous success. More people made decisions to follow Christ through that campaign by Dolores Catholic Church than any other church in the city of Austin. Our simple obedience made a huge difference in the lives of hundreds of families.

A Few Words on Worship
Throughout my life, I have enjoyed hunting. But I never expected God to come along with me! I mean, not in such a manner that I would be intensely aware of His Presence. Oddly enough, I know the Lord has used hunting trips as opportunities for worship. A holy transaction took place out in the

wild. God, the Father, used those times to let me speak to Him, and Him to me.

Now worship seems a simple enough word, although we don't use it much in conversation. The dictionary says to worship means "to revere, honor, or place in high esteem." If you think of this word at all, you may have an image of a "worship service" that takes place in a quiet building. Certainly, true worship may take place there, but the experiences I want to share speak of more.

There is something amazing about coming before the One, True, and Holy God and sensing His response to us. It may sound odd, but as human beings, we can bless God with our worship. We, mere humans, make God happy! On a bigger scale, it is a divine dialog, something like a good conversation with an old friend that brings joy to both parties.

The Tree

I had a profound experience in Colorado when I was in my mid forties that I remember clearly to this day. Of course, the views on the mountains are breathtaking to begin with. I sat on the side of a slope and looked across at the panorama before me. I was in a clearing with no trees on my right or left. There was no wind stirring, not even a breeze. I sat and drank in the beauty of God's creation and spoke to Him. The beauty of the landscape prompted worship. Creation speaks to us of a Creator.

Then suddenly, there was a whooshing sound behind me. As I turned, I saw a single aspen tree. Every leaf fell from that tree at once. In seconds, the tree that had been full of leaves stood bare. It was a sight to behold and I felt very close to God in that holy moment. If the tree could not stand in His Presence without being changed, neither could I.

The Snowfall

A few years later, I returned to Colorado with my son, Richard. It was the last day of hunting season, and we had not bagged a single deer. We were offered one last chance by a landowner to hunt on his property. As I walked along, I began to worship the Lord. It was not snowing one moment, and then it was the next. Soon it came down thick. A couple of inches gathered in thirty minutes or so.

"Well, Lord," I said, "I guess this is the end of my hunt, but I am going to praise You anyway." Then, it stopped just as quickly as it began. It was a glorious sight, white and silent, and I spoke to the Lord about the resplendent beauty of His creation. I had no candles, no instruments, no choir, no ceremony; nothing that you might think necessary for a worship service. I merely had my words and my heart to offer to the Lord. And then I was filled with a certainty that God had heard me in those intimate moments.

Suddenly, a buck appeared. He walked in my direction until he was only fifteen yards away. One tree stood between us. He passed on the other side of the tree. I raised my gun, shot at his neck and missed. Now even folks who do not hunt know that you must be quiet and still, or the intended targets will be gone in a flash. Deer have excellent eyesight; the smallest movement will frighten them. They react instantly at the slightest sound, such as the untimely snap of a twig.

This deer, however, did not run, not even at the resounding crack of my gun. In fact, he didn't look in my direction! I had to bring my gun down to reload; actions that took time and made noise. The deer was still walking. On my second shot, I got him. Because of the blanket of snow, I was able to pull him back to our truck about a half a mile away.

Once again, all the details had come together. I had opportunity to hunt on the last day of the season and had been in the right place at the moment the snow fell and the buck appeared. Why the buck did not run at the first shot or even look at me I cannot explain. I didn't feel lucky, I felt blessed. I am certain that God, the Almighty, was pleased with me and my simple worship. As a result, he saw fit to bless me. It is a very humbling thing.

Gratitude

In the 1980's, my son Bill and his buddies wanted to go elk hunting. A party of about ten young men planned a trip to Wyoming. I went along. We rented horses and set up a campsite about ten miles back into the wilderness.

On the opening morning of the season, I found a large rock outcropping not far from our campsite, and I sat down, resting my back against the rock. The scenery was something. It was so incredibly beautiful that I began to offer my praise to God for His amazing creation.

There were ridges sloping down in front of me. Each ridge had one slope with grass that rose to a point, and the alternate side was thick with trees. I could see grass, then trees, then grass and more trees. This beautiful pattern compelled me to worship all the more. I closed my eyes to concentrate on God. I sat for quite awhile. I cannot recall just how long I was there, but I remember staying for some length of time because I felt God's Presence. I knew somewhere deep in my soul that this was what we are made for, to commune with our Maker. It is a very fulfilling experience. After more time elapsed, I heard the phrase, "Thank you, Herman, now go hunting."

Can you imagine? God thanked me for my worship! As enjoyable as these moments were for me, I realized right then that the Lord enjoys our worship as well. It gives Him His rightful place in our thinking. Can you grasp this incredulous truth, that humans can bless God? I find this a mind-boggling concept, yet it is supposed to be this way. God enjoys us!

Just at this time, four elk came along, two cows and two calves to my right. Then I heard a bull off to my left. I turned to see him down the slope in a small clearing. I wanted to work my way down the slope, on the wooded side and come up on him from below. Suddenly I spotted another elk running at a considerable distance. In fact, I had to use the scope on my gun just to see if he had antlers. He did. I felt compelled to take the shot, yet I had turned down shots half that distance before. I got him! I am certain that is the longest shot I have ever made. Those were the last elk I saw in ten days of hunting. What an amazing opportunity.

I tear up when I think about how much God loves us. He uses the big life events as well as the small ones to speak to us about His majesty. It is remarkable that God speaks to us at all. On occasion, He uses hunting trips to do so.

Larry

I have met many remarkable people over my many years, but perhaps no one practices time in God's presence more than my friend, Larry Stokes. We have hosted a weekly prayer meeting in our home for over twelve years with members from five different churches. He has attended for some time now.

Larry has the most wonderful relationship with God that I have ever seen! He gets up at four o'clock each morning and prays and studies the Bible until seven. He plays worship tapes all day while he works. As a result of this devotion, I believe God speaks to him and blesses him often. Each week, all the members of our prayer group want to hear what God has said to Larry or done for him since we last met. Here are a few of the incredible things that he has experienced.

Larry was blind for twenty-six years from an explosion and learned to do upholstery work just by feel. God recently healed his sight, so he can now drive safely, read the Bible, and see all the beauty of God's creation. He is truly a walking testimony of God's grace concerning huge life-changing events, as well as the small details of daily life.

Larry needed a DVD player so he could watch his Christian videos, but he did not have the money to buy one. He knew that God told him to go to a store and choose a DVD player. He understood God to say He would give it to him. He obeyed, found the one he wanted, and just stood looking at it. A salesman came up and asked if he could help him. He said, "No, God is going to give me that DVD player." The salesman made some snide remark and left.

Larry stood there about twenty more minutes waiting on God. The salesman returned with a package in his hand and asked for forgiveness for his remark. "The man over there told me to give this to you," he said. It was the exact player he wanted. The person who had given the package to the store clerk was not there anymore. Could it have been an angel?

Larry worked for an upholstery company in Marble Falls, Texas, when a company in his hometown of Kingsland contacted him and gave him an offer for a job. He started doing part time work for the company in Kingsland, since the company in Marble Falls didn't have much work and he was paid per job rather than by the hour.

A short time later, the Marble Falls man called and said he had more work to do and asked Larry to come back full time. Larry didn't have peace about the job in Marble Falls, but didn't feel he could hear what God's will was. He decided to go back to the Marble Falls job.

He was in his truck early the next morning in a filling station in Kingsland, having a cup of coffee, when a total stranger walked up with his Bible open and read him John 15, verse 5, "I am the vine and you are the branches." Then the stranger said, "God sent me to tell you He has provided the job for you here in Kingsland and you are to stay here." The man that God sent to give Larry that message was from Florida. He just happened to be visiting his family in Johnson City, about thirty-five miles from Kingsland.

God recently told Larry to rent a certain house to live in instead of the mobile home where he was living. The house did not have any furniture. A couple had just purchased a house next to ours. They had recently married, and each had a complete set of furniture. When they heard that Larry needed furniture, they gave him everything he needed to fully furnish his house, including a washer and dryer.

Larry works repairing furniture and other items in a large warehouse. One day, he was all by himself, and he opened a huge twelve foot by twelve foot metal door. As he was standing there, it fell on him. He raised his hands to catch it. Feeling the weight of the door totally crushing him, he said, "God, please help me put the door back." God set it back right where and how it should be. Later a man asked how he got it back up, since it took four men to put it up when the building was constructed originally.

That night was our weekly prayer meeting, and Larry came, even though he needed help walking into our house.

We all prayed for him and took Communion together, and God instantly healed him. After a few minutes, God told Larry to get up and walk. He was walking and leaping and praising God!

This should prove to all of us that the most profitable thing we can ever do is stay in His presence, loving and worshipping Him. Practicing God's presence was something I would learn more about, but it took many years to grasp. I let other passions dilute my highest calling, to worship God above all else.

Windermere Oaks

Remember, my passion for the real estate business was growing. One venture just seemed to give way to another.

About the time we finished selling at Rolling Oaks Ranch, I had a gentleman ask me if I would be interested in some property along Lake Travis. His sister owned about three hundred acres with over a mile of lake frontage.

"What is she asking for it?"

"Three hundred dollars an acre," he said.

He had my attention. I went to see the property. I had an attorney friend who served as a financial investor and he wanted in as well.

I spoke with the owner, and we agreed to her selling price. We were set to sign a contract the day after next, but the owner called me with a problem.

"I am sorry, but I just can't take three hundred per acre for that."

"What do you have to have?" I asked.

"Four hundred per acre."

I told her I would talk to my partner. We all agreed on that price, and that we would close the day after tomorrow. The day arrived, and she called again.

"I cannot take that price. I need five hundred per acre." I agreed, and we had an appointment to sign the documents.

Would you believe, she called a third time? "I am so sorry, but I just cannot sell at that price. I would need six hundred per acre."

"Well, I hope you get it," was all I said and hung up decisively.

I waited about a month without contacting the owner. Then I conferred with my partner. "You know, six hundred an acre was a reasonable price." He agreed.

We called the lady and offered her that price. "But not one penny more," I insisted. At last, the deal was signed and we set out to develop the subdivision.

I named it Windermere Oaks. The roads and water system went in, and soon enough, we were selling land. I was determined to sell as much as I could, so I looked for creative ways to draw in new clients. Our fourth child, Gay, tells her story of assisting me.

"I will never forget the summer I was seventeen years old and Dad gave me a job. He had a notebook with photos of his properties, and I would take that book and go door to door showing people what he had to offer. I had the responsibility of making appointments for Dad if they showed interest. I was so good at this that he named me The Best Sales Person Ever, and he paid me seventeen dollars per hour. Some people would not think to have a teenager sell real estate door to door, but Dad had unique ways of doing things."

As the paperwork mounted, I had a young CPA named Don Hart keeping track of all the financial records, and I soon made him my partner. An investor in Houston asked to buy the remaining part of the subdivision. Don and I went to see our potential buyer and settled on a deal that promised us a considerable figure. With a sizable note on the Windermere properties, I looked for larger stakes. After all, God was at work in the details of my life both large and small, and I was on a mission to sell land.

Chapter Eight
Two Million in Debt

SOME TRUST IN CHARIOTS AND SOME IN HORSES,
BUT WE TRUST IN THE NAME OF THE LORD OUR GOD.
PSALM 20:7

Personal Property

Opportunity knocked at my door again. The first chance to increase my holdings was to purchase a thousand-acre ranch near Davilla, Texas, which is northeast of Georgetown. The property had two thirty-acre lakes and a dozen or so catfish ponds. I named it the Rocking N Ranch. It was perfect for raising cattle, so rather than developing the land, I set out to buy cows. I hired a fellow named Joe Frerick to run the ranch. I decided to buy Chianina (Kee-a-nee-na) cattle; an old breed, large and hearty, that came from Italy.

I needed financing to invest in cattle and found my way to the Bryan Production Credit Association, BPCA. But I needed more collateral than my land. Joe approached a friend, Tommy Hagelin, who worked as a county agent. His mother put up her home and farm to secure my loan. My ranch was turning into quite a venture. Although BPCA was a small lending institution and my loan was sizable, we were set.

Fairway Farm

I was driven to buy and sell more land, and a prime prospect came along in the form of a beautiful development near San Augustine called Fairway Farm. It was situated in the woods of East Texas and featured a huge home, two championship golf courses, and a conference center. It even had its own airstrip. The owner's mansion had something like fourteen bedrooms.

The widow of the owner wanted to sell for a million dollars in cash. I had not seen it yet, but on the recommendations of others and some photographs I had seen, I called and offered to buy it. I had to put down fifty thousand. That required borrowing from a bank. With a ninety day contract, I had to come up with nine hundred, fifty thousand dollars right quick.

The banker who put up the first of the cash asked to see Fairway Farm, and since I had been able to buy a little Cessna plane, we flew out to there. As much as he liked the property, he was skeptical that I could raise the rest of the money. He said, "If you can come up with that much that fast, you will make a believer out of me." I tried several avenues, but nothing turned up.

Finally, I went to the Bishop's office to ask if the Bishop would want to invest. A priest there told me about an effort in Waco to build a Catholic High School. He recommended I speak with them. The priest in Waco and his attorney asked to see Fairway Farm as well. They were quite impressed, but did not have the resources I needed. However, they reported what they had seen to the Bishop and encouraged him to invest. He took their endorsement, and by selling bonds, he was able to come up with the one million. That made us equal partners in a deal that looked more than promising.

I hired a fellow to call on major corporations that might want to use the beautiful facilities at Fairway. Several companies decided to hold their Board of Directors meetings in that location. As businessmen came to Fairway Farm, they asked me about subdividing the property, but the Bishop felt it should be sold as a whole. Word spread and we had interest from investors in Florida who came to see the site and offered to buy at a two million profit, so we had a twenty-page contract drawn up. To say the least, it was very detailed and quite secure. The

Bishop and I would each make a million dollars. On the basis of that contract, I was ecstatic.

Explosive Growth

I signed another contract on a huge ranch east of Dallas with a hundred and fifty-acre lake and several nice homes. I needed one hundred thousand dollars down on this million-dollar deal. I approached another bank I had not dealt with before, and they were quite willing to lend me the money. I soon had a contract that assured me another half a million in profit.

I suppose you could say I was spellbound by this apparent success and went wild signing deals in New Mexico: one for sixty-five thousand acres, one for fifty thousand, and a small one for just thirty-five thousand acres. I signed three contracts. I fully expected to make a million dollars on Fairway Farm and another half a million on the property east of Dallas and that would, in turn, serve me in buying the land in New Mexico.

The Crash

In a very short span, every contract I had failed. The offer on the Dallas area property fell through. The Florida investors with the contract on Fairway Farm were caught in the 1980's credit crisis of the Savings and Loan industry. With no way to borrow enough money, that contract collapsed. Suddenly I was two million in debt. It had all caught up with me, and there were no ready solutions. I had people working for me, but I had to close the office. One day, I was so totally exhausted, I drove home, crawled into bed, and slept for twenty-four hours straight. When I woke up, I realized what a miserable life I was living.

I came to the Lord. "Please forgive me for this," I said. "I want to give you the rest of my life, but if you want me to die this second, take me." I kept breathing. In fact, the incredible weight that had been crushing me was gone. There is no explanation for this, but I felt totally at peace even though I did not know how to fix my situation. I would just have to wait, trust, and see what God would do. My life, including my financial problem, was in His hands.

God's Way Out

Short of receiving Christ, being thrown into two million in debt was one of the best things that ever happened to me. I had used a thousand percent of my energy on business dealings and making money, but debt changed everything. I became totally dependent on the Lord, and I knew it. I desperately needed divine intervention, and that is just what I got.

After surrendering myself to God and asking for his mercy, I received a notice from the Bryan Production Credit Association informing me that the ranch in Davilla was in jeopardy. Sometimes things get worse before they get better, and although it is an effective reminder that we are not in control, at the time this news did not seem one bit helpful or encouraging.

The BPCA needed me to pay my note within thirty days or lose the collateral. That meant that I would lose Rocking N Ranch, my cattle, and the property owned by the Hagelins. They were all at risk. The credit association explained that my loan was so large, it could put them out of business if it failed. As a result, they required me to pay in full in thirty days.

I needed a miracle. I made a few attempts to find people with the means to help me. I found a gentleman who offered to put up assets so I could keep my loan. He was scheduled to go with me to speak to the BPCA. This looked like the beginning of a way out. The day came that I had to meet with the loan officer. I went to pick up the financial partner to make our trip to Bryan, but as it turned out, he was not home, and had called to say he could not go. Apparently, he had his own pressing business matters to attend to, so I suggested that I should meet with the creditors anyway and he agreed. I needed another plan, and I needed it right away.

Tommy Hagelin and I drove to Bryan. I thought of any possible options for keeping the loan. I found an old envelope and began to jot down notes. What if we subdivided the property, as I had done before with other ranches, and sold lots to be developed? The buyers could make payments directly to the BPCA. Yet I knew full well that the BPCA only granted loans for agricultural purposes, so this proposal would likely fall on deaf ears.

I expected to sit down with the loan officer. Instead, we were ushered into a large conference room where we met the entire Board of Directors. I offered my proposal about dividing the ranch. I asked the fateful questions. Would they let me do this? How much money down would they require? The chairman, Dowell Hailey, turned to another director who had been a realtor.

"Do you think this will work?"

"Yes, I know darn well it will work."

There was my answer. They agreed to extend the loan, not cancel it. God had literally saved my farm and the Hagelin's farm as well.

I was greatly relieved. We started to leave when Mr. Hailey said, "Herman, wait. We've forgotten something."

I thought, "Oh no, this is it. Our deal is falling through after all."

"You are going to need money to develop the place. How much do you think it will take?"

He was right. We sat down again and discussed amounts for roads, a full water system, and surveying. He said, "Well, we'll lend you that amount, too."

Remember, I was two million in debt. This was not normal business practice. This was a huge miracle, and it had just grown into a larger one! What I did not know at the time of this meeting was that one of the first people I spoke to about helping with my debt had attempted to cut me out of the deal altogether.

Apparently, after seeing the land and all that was at stake, he had gone to the head of the BPCA and offered to buy my note in full. Had they taken his offer, I would have lost everything. Now, it might have been a great deal for the credit association, but instead of taking the fellow's payment, they came to me and offered me thirty days to pay up. I had no idea this offer had been made behind the scenes, but once I heard about it, I realized all the more how the Lord protected me and provided for me once again. If you ask anyone in the real estate and financial business world, they will tell you how incredible their offer to me was. This was absolutely nothing short of a miracle.

Westridge

I set to work. We divided the Rocking N Ranch to sell five-acre tracts. Buyers made their monthly payments to the BPCA, and over a few years, all that I owed them was paid in full.

Mr. Hailey contacted me a year or so later with another business proposal. He had a thousand-acre ranch he owned north of Temple, Texas, and he wanted me to develop the property. Apparently he liked the outcome of our first deal and he trusted me enough to oversee another development that would turn his raw ranch land into home sites.

Now keep in mind, at the time of his proposal, I had not completely cleared the two million dollars in debt I had incurred. Mr. Hailey sought me out and offered me some very generous terms for this new project. First, he offered to sell me the land for five hundred per acre when we both knew it was worth about seven hundred and fifty an acre. He also lent me seventy-five thousand to develop the property, covering the surveys and road construction. Then, he allowed me to assign contracts to him as the subdivided lots sold. That was my only way to repay the new loan. All I had to offer was my service and I was willing to give it. I believe that God used Mr. Hailey as a means for my economic recovery.

I named the subdivision Westridge and put my energy into it. I sold our home on Pineleaf Place in Austin and moved out to the development that was situated between the towns of Eddy and Moody, Texas. I put a mobile home out there, and Zita and our youngest daughter Mary joined me as I worked diligently to sell lots. There wasn't much out there in those days, except for one other subdivision that featured a swimming pool and tennis courts. The realtors for the competition ran a full-page ad enticing folks to enjoy country living.

The odd thing was, I had nothing to compare with such amenities. I ran a meager fifteen-word ad in a few newspapers and as a result, I had many people come to look at the properties in Westridge even though they had to drive right by the more developed community. Those "lookers" became buyers, and Westridge outsold the competition. This may all seem contrary to sound business logic, but I see it as God's hand and his way of moving me out of debt.

Divorce

Perhaps the only thing more complicated than debt is divorce. Zita and I reached an impasse. She had traveled to a foreign country many times to pursue an Eastern religion and she planned to go again. I sensed very deeply that the Lord said she should not go. The love for her that I received at Camps Farthest Out had lasted for twenty-five years, but now it was time to speak up. Although I knew my insistence would be hard for both of us, I was compelled to take a stand, so I did, and Zita left. Our marriage of forty-two years came to an end.

Chapter Nine
The Most Blessed Man on Earth

O LORD ALMIGHTY,
BLESSED IS THE MAN WHO TRUSTS IN YOU.
PSALM 84:12

If you ask me how I'm doing, I usually reply, "I think I am the most blessed man on earth."

This is not merely a snappy phrase; I truly feel that way. I know some would say debt and divorce are more hardships than blessings. But these are the types of challenges that life is made of, and I believe they are incredible opportunities to see God. Besides, I cannot count my hardships as outweighing the blessing of knowing Christ and being filled with a tremendous love from Jesus and for Jesus.

The number one reason I feel so blessed sounds rather simple, but it is deeply profound: I understand that God loves me. He has taken every speck of sin and debt from me. I stand clean before Him because of the sacrifice of Jesus upon the cross. I know God's love for me is deep and intense and, as a result, so is mine for Him.

Legacy

Aside from receiving the transforming love of Christ, my greatest blessings are the children God gave to Zita and me. I must say that I will always respect Zita for the role she played in raising our children. They have strength of character that does not come accidentally. All six of them are dynamic individuals and successful in their own right.

Donna, the Businesswoman

Our oldest child, Donna Ruth, was born in the first year of our marriage and named for our close friends Don and Ruth Sullivan.

"Donna really is just so savvy," says Zita. "She has this complex brain that makes her a tremendous problem solver. Donna is a beautiful woman in body and spirit. She is compassionate and witty and I treasure her friendship."

Donna holds a PhD in Educational Psychology from The University of Texas at Austin. She was a vice president of Tellabs, Inc. for five years before she started her own consulting business and was hired by major corporations all across the U.S.

Donna wrote a book called *The High Performance Enterprise: Reinventing the People Side of Your Business*. It proved so valuable, a second edition was published five years after the first.

I did not pay for her to go to college. She paid her own way. In fact, all of my children had to do that, since I was working my way out of considerable debt during many of those years.

She has been a partner with Cyndi Harris for eleven years. Donna and Cyndi are both quite gifted and wonderful people. They have helped us considerably with our work in Haiti regarding many organizational decisions. Beyond the pride I feel at Donna's business success, words cannot express how much I love her.

Richard, the Pastor

Our second child is Richard Clayton. He received his master's degree from Southwest Baptist Theological Seminary in Ft. Worth where he met his precious wife, Sylvia, who also received her master's degree there. After graduating, he became a pastor, serving in two churches over nine years in the state of Washington. They moved back to Austin, and he is the pastor of True Life Fellowship in Round Rock, Texas.

Zita says Richard is outgoing, "but not the total extrovert his Dad is. He has a sweet, softer side to his character. I feel that his selflessness helps to make him a genuinely exceptional pastor."

He and Sylvia have two remarkable children. Adrienne graduated from Texas A&M in 2006 with a degree in Spanish. She has tutored inner city kids at the Austin Opportunity Center and has made a three-year commitment to foreign missions where she is currently serving. Jared also graduated from Texas A&M. He has served as a youth pastor and currently attends a school for ministry at Bethel Church in Redding, California.

Esta, the Realtor and Artist

Esta Ann is our third child. Zita recently stayed with Esta for eight months to help her with cancer treatments. Zita said, "We had such a good time together. I know chemo is not usually associated with fun. But we have such good rapport. I do with all of my adult children."

Esta says Mom went with her for most of the treatments. "She brought me soup or juice and pillows. She put socks on my feet and tucked them into the blanket. We played cards and laughed together. We fell in love while I was hooked up and helpless." Esta reports that on the very morning of her diagnosis, she heard the Lord speak through verses in Deuteronomy that he would be with her in battle and not to be afraid.

Like any Dad would be, I am so pleased to see my daughter's great strength and this bond with her mother. I am also overjoyed to say that the treatment worked and, by God's grace, Esta is cancer free.

As for Esta and me, we traveled together to Israel some years ago. I had the privilege of baptizing her in the Jordan River. It was one of those memorable life events that you carry in your mind and heart forever.

You might say Esta has followed a family tradition into real estate. She is quite a multi-faceted person, also having a considerable talent for art. She is married to John Ingle, who is a systems engineer for Dell. They had four talented sons: Joshua, Daniel, Thomas and James. Their first son, Josh, experienced an untimely death at the age of twenty-one.

Daniel is hardworking and artistic. He is polite and reliable and quite good with his hands. He and Nicole have one little girl named Kailee.

Thomas, like his grandfather, likes to fish. He is a fisher of men as well. At his public high school, he posed a challenge to his football team that had begun another losing season. He asked his teammates to pray with him before and after each game. This simple act of humility, to honor God, brought change. That was the first year their team had a winning season. It changed the effectiveness of the team from that time on.

James, their youngest, has a sharp sense of humor to go along with his outgoing personality. He is a crafter of words, is musically inclined, and has the gift of compassion.

Gay, the Sensitive Seller

Zita Gay is our fourth child, named after her mother, who says that Gay is one of the sweetest people you could meet. "Gay is Miss Delightful, in many ways. She is the most selfless, positive and patient person, always working to benefit others. And, much like her dad, she is quite outgoing. We managed to have a few extroverts in our family."

Gay is married to Mickey Harris. You could say they have a ministry of helping others. They began a youth basketball association in Thorndale, Texas, and worked together for the Down Home Ranch, a facility for special needs children.

"Mickey has been a salesman for many products, but mainly he helps other people start up a business, and once it gets going, he moves on to the next one," explains Gay.

Gay and Mickey have five children: Chris, Ann, Jonathan, Todd and Mickey. The Harris's homeschooled back when it was not so fashionable, and their commitment to the kids' education paid off with many accomplishments.

Their oldest, Chris, is described as full of wisdom and is tenderhearted. He attended Law School at Baylor. He is married to Sarah, also a lawyer, and they have a precious little one named Adelynn Grace.

Ann is a servant leader. She recently married Michael Zernial. She is a nurse, a massage therapist and a teacher. Currently she teaches Medical Technologies at a local high school. Ann served on a medical mission to Ethiopia where she lived at a remote clinic for three months.

Jonathan and his young bride Dawn Ashley attend UT and are studying abroad. He, too, has the hunting and fishing gene from his grandfather. He loves life, truth, and practical jokes.

Todd, also attending UT, has a very active sense of humor. He is an amazing musician; he plays the drums as well as acoustic and electric guitar. He has played in bands and church worship teams. Todd has a great rapport with children.

Mickey, who is in high school, is a thinker and a loyal friend and brother. He is fun-loving and outgoing. He plans to go to UT also and major in business.

Bill, the Fence Builder

Our fifth child, William Herman, goes by Bill. He gave us more problems in his teen years than all the other children combined. How God has changed him! The Lord is using Bill to serve His purposes. I think that is due to the fact that Bill listens to God, spending considerable time each day in prayer and Bible study. In fact, I am quite convinced that the Lord uses Bill in supernatural ways as a direct result of Bill's commitment to come before Him.

Bill has been involved in several mission efforts and recently went with me to Haiti. He runs a group of businesses including Foundation Fence. He has been recognized for many of his fence designs, including a type of barrier for highway medians.

"Bill can wear twelve hats," Zita says. "He can work very hard, doing many different things at once. But for all that hard work, he likes to have fun. He has a big heart."

Bill and his wife Agnes have five children. Stephen is the oldest. He and his wife Cristina have three children: Celeste, Stevie and Joshua. Stephen saw a miracle occur when his business partner fell very ill. The fellow's heart stopped for an hour, yet began to beat again after Bill prayed for him.It sounds incredible, yet my grandson can tell you it is true. An absolute miracle occurred when Bill prayed because God was gracious.

Paul, Bill's second child, attends college and is working full time. He is well traveled; he has been with me to Haiti and has served in China. He is pursuing an English degree and wants to work in foreign missions.

Sarah also has a desire to return to China since she visited there on a mission trip. She recently graduated from Texas A&M and intends to work in international commerce in China and perhaps North Korea.

Elizabeth, who is called Izzy, served as my partner on the mission trip to Eastern Europe. She is in college and wants to pursue a career that will benefit children.

Rounding out the family is William, adopted from Korea and now a high school student who excels in soccer. He also plays in the Central Texas Honor Band.

Mary, the Nurse

Our youngest, Mary Theresa, is a geriatric nurse practitioner. In high school, she had a part time job in a nursing home where she realized her great interest in working with elderly people.

Zita says, "I see Mary as unique, perhaps because she is my baby. She is her own person, quite fun-loving. She encourages us to do silly things, like arranging for the sisters to go to the movies. We all came out singing. She is full of inner and outer beauty and grace."

Mary has been to Haiti twice where she served many needy people. She waited until her forties for the right fellow. She found him in Bob Mann, who is a paramedic with Williamson County EMS. This is the first marriage for both of them. I could not be more proud of these two.

Do you begin to see how tremendously God has blessed me? In addition to God given talents and tenacity, the legacy of faith continues in my grandchildren. I am deeply grateful.

Joys and Sorrows

After my divorce, I attended a Christian conference in Idaho. One of the speakers was a widow named Liz Johnson. As she was speaking,

I clearly understood that God was saying to me, "This is the one I have for you."

I had moved to Hoover Valley, just outside of Burnet, Texas. Liz came down to central Texas to visit her daughter, and we got to know one another better. She confirmed what I had heard at the conference.

In 1992, at sixty-seven, I began my second marriage. I must admit that the first few years were difficult. It was an adjustment for both of us, and as I look back, I realize that God was at work then to prepare me for the future.

Within a few years, Liz had two strokes. She needed help dressing and bathing, especially after the second one. I devoted my time to caring for her.

One day late in the year of 1999, Liz told me that it was time for me to go back into ministry. I wondered how that would be possible, given her need for daily care. Not long after that, we held our usual Thursday night prayer meeting in our home. We sang the hymn "Holy, Holy, Holy." Liz commented that she loved that song so much she hoped to include it in her funeral.

The next day we had a head-on car wreck that killed the man who hit us. I remember certain images, such as lying on the ground and not being able to move. I called out to Liz, but she did not answer. I was in bad shape. A man stopped to help us, and I remember talking to him. I also remember that the pain was intense. I had been a volunteer ambulance driver and knew what my pain was telling me. I had a severe head injury, broken ribs and a fractured left leg.

I was taken to the Burnet Hospital ER where I was told that Liz had not survived. One of my greatest concerns at that time was for Liz's daughter, Sue. She would be deeply affected by the loss of her mother. But when she came to see me at the Burnet Hospital, she told me that she would be all right, because the Lord had showed her recently that He would be taking her mom to heaven soon. It is hard to explain just how relieved I was to hear this.

They loaded me back in an ambulance and sent me to an Austin hospital. I had a paramedic friend ride with me. He confirmed that my left leg was broken between my knee and my ankle. I know that my children and grandchildren were praying for me, and in the course of that ambulance ride, my leg was healed. I went into the ambulance one way and came out another; the fracture no longer existed. All I know is that God was at work. It is not up to us to decide when and how our lives end or how healing comes. I had been spared a fatal accident as an infant back in the 1920's, and I was spared once again.

Since I was not fully aware of all that went on around me, I will let my granddaughter, Adrienne, tell you the story in her words. She would have been a teenager at the time.

A Granddaughter's Story

"I watched my mother's grave expression while she talked to my Aunt Agnes on the phone; I could tell the news was bad -- real bad -- because of my mom's response. My stomach was in knots. Finally, my mom hung up.

'Your Papa and Grandma Liz were in an accident,' she said. 'The man who witnessed the wreck says that Papa will probably make it, but he is not so sure Liz will.'

"I was stunned. A few minutes later, my aunt called back. Grandma Liz had passed away. I wasn't sure what to do. My dad and brother were driving home from a football game. We made plans to head straight to the hospital as soon as Dad and Jared came home.

"As we drove up, an ambulance was pulling away, and we discovered later it was taking Papa to a hospital in Austin. Not a lot was said; there were lots of hugs and tears though. I watched my dad and his brother Bill hold each other tight. I would have never thought that two men who seemed so strong could cry so hard. This was the first time death had touched our family.

"The next afternoon, we went down to visit Papa in ICU. We were notified that his major injuries included a crushed sternum, many broken ribs, internal bleeding in his head, and a concussion. In other words, lots of pain. Since Papa had six children, it was awhile before all the grandkids were allowed to see him. By the time it was our turn, the nurse said he needed rest. But we didn't let that stop us. All the grandkids filed in and prayed for Papa behind the glass window. Because Papa requested it, we were allowed to go in and talk with him. One by one, we took hold of his outstretched hand as he would tell us what a blessing we were and how much he loved us.

"Grandma Liz's funeral was on Wednesday, and because Papa was still too critical to come, we went straight to his hospital room afterwards to give him a full report. He wanted to know every detail, so my mom and I tried to sing him one of the songs. I say we tried to sing, because we sang while watching Papa weep uncontrollably as he experienced great sorrow.

"Despite the extraordinary pain, physical and emotional, Papa appeared to think nothing of himself. Everyone who knew him was touched that week by his loving words and by his tears.

"I don't know that I've ever seen a man cry so much in one week. But they were not tears of suffering and grief. They were tears of joy. I probably heard him say a hundred times, 'I am the most blessed man in the whole world.' Then I would look around at the machines, IV's, and tubes hooked up to him and wonder, what if I were in his shoes? Would I be able to say the same thing? I still am amazed that this old man who was staring death square in the face could have such peace. He learned to be content, regardless of the circumstances. God was by his side, and that was enough for him.

"Several weeks later, he was well enough to get around, and we had a memorial service in honor of Grandma Liz. Papa shared something that touched every heart in the room. Instead of being filled with remorse, he was overflowing with joy. He had an increased measure of faith because he knew that his life was completely in God's hands. Papa gave a challenge to all of us: don't wait to give up everything to follow Jesus. Do it now. He told us how important it was to live for eternity. Would we live for ourselves, or for God? He told us to choose what really matters."

Mission Revived

When I was released from the hospital in early 2000, my youngest daughter Mary came to live with me for a month. Because of her medical knowledge, my youngest child was the best person to stay with me. I had a fairly smooth recovery with one exception. A few months after the accident, I had trouble buttoning my shirt. My coordination was off.

I made an appointment to see a doctor. He was not overly concerned, yet the problem did not go away. I went to see a second doctor with the same result. At that time, Mary absolutely insisted that I have an MRI. She would not relent, and her perseverance turned out to be a good thing. The result of the test caused enough alarm that I was sent to a hospital immediately.

I had a broken blood vessel in my head that caused so much pressure that it had pushed my brain to the side. I was told that had it been any worse, I would have stopped breathing. Once again, the Lord showed his faithfulness to me. The surgery to repair the broken vessel left a dent in my skull, but no other physical signs of my traumatic wreck remain. The greatest mark was on my soul; I gained a renewed passion for following Christ.

Venturing Out

My recovery was so successful that by May, I was asked to go along with Bill and some of his family on a mission trip to Hungary. Robert Vidaurri, a contact of Bill's and now an employee, had a great deal of experience leading teams on mission trips. Robert led twenty-six U.S. citizens on this adventure through an organization called Mission Netcast. We went to a small town called Elek in the southern part of Hungary, near the Romanian border. The people in the area are Gypsies, which despite some misconceptions, are their own ethnic group.

Our goal was to share our faith with as many people as we could by walking through neighborhoods and knocking on doors. We went out in pairs along with a Hungarian translator. My granddaughter Izzy was my partner. She was eleven years old at the time and I was seventy-five. I think we made quite a team.

Moved by Miracles

My son Bill has been to that same village a few times and has experienced amazing things. During our first trip, we had a large tent set up to hold meetings. At one of those meetings, a woman asked if we would come to the hospital to pray for her infant who was quite ill. Bill was one of the key people who prayed for the baby, and the baby was healed!

The lady reported to her community of friends, and soon we had mothers and children gathering for prayer. Every one of these precious little ones was healed. As vitally important as these miracles were to the families, they also spoke to the entire community of God's unlimited power. Over two hundred people among the Gypsies came to place their trust and faith in Christ.

On a return trip, they asked Bill to come to the children's hospital to pray. One of the young teenaged girls needed a bone marrow transplant for leukemia. Bill and the group prayed fervently for the girl. Three days later the girl was well enough to be released from the hospital. Her disease was gone!

What stands out to me is the quantity of time Bill spends in study and prayer. He does not do so merely to gain power. He desires to be in God's presence and one of the outcomes is the working of miracles.

The trip was a marvelous success in many ways and it served to link my past and my future. I had learned about witnessing door to door in my days at Dolores Catholic Church, and there I was, doing the same sort of thing half a world away. Also, it made me think about what I would do next. Was there another mission ahead of me?

Liz had said that I should return to ministry. Two months after that mission trip, in July of 2000, some friends came to visit and introduced me to a pastor from Haiti. On that very day, my neighbor arrived with an interesting device called a solar cooker. The details and the timing could not be ignored. Once again, the Lord was calling me to a mission.

Chapter Ten
Fellowship, Family, Fishing, and Fortune

WE PROCLAIM TO YOU WHAT WE HAVE SEEN AND HEARD, SO
THAT YOU ALSO MAY HAVE FELLOWSHIP WITH US.
I JOHN 1:3

One of the many blessings of the Christian life is attending church. It is one of the key places that we draw near to the Lord. We can listen and learn, relate to others, and serve. I have had the privilege of attending a few churches where I have learned a great deal about following Christ.

Catholic Roots

I will say that in my early years, I didn't think too much about my faith. My father was a Catholic, and I went to Mass with him. I think it was a given in those days that people believed in God. But I also knew some folks had a serious devotion to their faith that was seen in their actions. My Aunt Katie went to the Catholic Church in St. Francis every day, as I recall. She told me that she prayed for me, and I believed then, as I do now, that something significant was prompted by those prayers.

When I was in the Navy, I told you how I went to Mass every day. I am completely convinced that the frequency and consistency of my attendance saved me from moral impurity and all manner of ruin. I do not take that purity for granted. I know I was much like any other young man in the Navy in WWII. It was the Lord who protected me. And strength came to me through the Mass.

I believe my true moment of conversion came during the Cursillo, or short course, offered through the Austin Diocese while I was a member of St. Louis. During some of my years there, I also attended the weeknight prayer meeting at Dolores Catholic Church. It was an exciting and dynamic time when I learned a great deal. I learned about hearing God speak and how to share my faith with others. While others may be inclined to criticize the Catholic Church for theological shortcomings, I have a great respect for my deep spiritual roots. I grew closer to God, and I was affirmed in my belief that we take our blessings and use what we are given to serve others, including the poor.

Finding Fellowship

When I moved out to Westridge, I lived out in the country, south of Waco. I needed a local church, one I could participate in regularly without commuting to Austin. I think Mary may have introduced me to Solomon's Porch, a nondenominational church outside of Temple, Texas. I felt very close to the Lord and felt he spoke to me about several important issues while I attended there. It was clear to me that the Lord was allowing me to grow. I had to trust Him with every part of my life, including my financial recovery.

Once I moved to Davilla, I attended the local Assembly of God Church. I would say that I felt at ease in both Catholic and Protestant churches by then. The name on the sign was not what was most important. What stood out the most to me was continuity. We must stay connected with other believers, and we must continue to hear good teaching. If you or I stop attending church, we will quickly grow spiritually stale. Sadly, that can happen without us noticing. The simple solution is to stay fresh by gathering regularly with other believers.

Different Dynamics

When I moved to Hoover Valley, near Burnet, I joined Anchor of Hope Church in Marble Falls where I attended for fifteen years. I believe that church attendance is more than showing up on

Sunday morning. To be active in the ongoing life and ministry of a church requires serving. For ten years I was able to serve as an elder there.

During this time, a Christian men's movement called Promise Keepers extended its influence into Central Texas. The group was characterized by unity across generations, races, and denominations. I attended three of their rallies and participated in a pastors' conference sponsored by Promise Keepers. I went to Washington D.C. in 1997 for the Million Man March, which is reported to be the single largest Christian men's gathering in history.

There is something powerful about coming together in such a large group. Some have said that men have been in the background of the church in America. The stereotype that Christian faith is something for women could not be better dispelled than by that sort of gathering. It was thrilling to see more than a million men in one place at one time with the single purpose of honoring God. As the Promise Keepers say, "Real men love Jesus."

While attending Anchor of Hope, I became very aware of the power and necessity of prayer. I began a Thursday night prayer meeting at my home about twelve years ago that continues today. We have extended our circle to include folks from several churches. Our common thread is our love for Jesus Christ and our desire to bring needs to Him in prayer.

Recently, I began attending Hill Country Fellowship in Burnet, which is experiencing explosive growth. We have three services on Sunday. I can say that it is very focused upon Christ and that I love it more than any church I have ever attended. There is quality teaching from the leaders and enthusiasm among the congregation. Just one of the outcomes of these things is a trip we are planning to take volunteers to Haiti.

Family and a Fish Tale

As I reflect on my roots, I know the importance of my parents' roles. While I was busy developing real estate in Central Texas, my parents were moving on in years up in the Panhandle.

Dad came to visit me on one occasion and, of course, I took him fishing. We went out for white bass at a nearby lake. You can gain a good indication of where the fish are by watching the gulls diving down toward the surface. They are feeding on shad, which also draws the bigger fish. I saw the seagulls working, so we went to that spot and caught six or seven fish right away. When the fish quit biting,

I knew the school had moved on. I saw the birds working the surface about a quarter of a mile away. I told Dad it was time to move the boat because we needed to go where the birds were. He asked, "What's wrong with this spot?"

We caught a few more fish on the second stop, but soon enough I saw the birds about a half-mile down the lake. It was time to pick up the anchor and go. But Dad wanted to know once again, "What's wrong with this place?"

A Life Well Lived

My folks eventually divorced, and my dad moved into Amarillo when he retired. He worked a few days a week at the St. Vincent DePaul Thrift Store. One day when he was alone in the store, he drifted off to sleep. Robbers came in and hit him on the head, knocking him out. Arnold reported to me that they had broken Dad's jaw and it had to be wired shut for some time to mend. After that, Dad developed a serious case of gout. His condition grew worse and we had him checked by several doctors.

Dad went into the hospital and was taken off the gout medicine. That brought improvement. However, he was hooked to a heart monitor and grew increasingly frightened. Arnold asked him what the trouble was, and Dad said he was concerned that the monitor displayed a line zigzagging up and down. He thought the line should be consistent and straight. Arnold explained that a straight line would mean that he was dead!

Dad was born in 1895, and ninety years later, he passed on. I can say that he was a wonderful and giving man. He worked very hard when he had the opportunity, and he loved his children.

A Word about Mom

My mother lived for years after Dad passed. My daughters tell of the opportunity they took to visit her.

"I recall Grandmother rocking my children," says Esta. "She would tell stories of nursing her own babies. I certainly recall that she did not worry about a clean house! And she always had Chihuahuas. She loved those little dogs and wanted a house full of them."

Sometime in about 1998, I got a call from my brother and sister. My mother had come to the point of needing daily care. I went up to Amarillo to help my family move her into a nursing home. She had started attending church, and we were happy to know that she had come to faith. I admit that we had to trick her into going to visit the home. But once she realized that the staff would take care of her, she adjusted to her surroundings. About a year later, Mother passed on. I know she had a very hard life, and I am deeply grateful that she now has an eternity to enjoy in heaven.

Friendship: Finding Janet

Almost forty years ago I had a pleasant encounter with a couple that became limited partners with me in a real estate transaction. I had maintained contact with Janet and Buck Redding over the years through that real estate partnership. I was aware that Buck had been killed in a car wreck and that Janet had remained single for eight years. I was recovering well from my own wreck and progressing through the grief process of losing Liz.

I called up Janet one day and asked if she would like to have lunch the next time I came into town from my house out in the country. She was eager to do so, but I did not make the trip for several weeks. Eventually, I found that I needed to buy a copier, and that meant a trip into Austin. We had lunch that day, and I managed to come back into town quite often after that!

It is easy to run out of adjectives when describing Janet. She is a very engaging and godly woman. We share many common experiences in our Christian walk. We have enjoyed the same retreat center over the years and have many mutual friends. Added to that, we share a serious commitment to missions. We were married in 2001, and Janet has been on all but one of my trips to Haiti since then. When I tell folks that I am the most blessed man on earth, she is a very large part of that answer. The Lord could not have brought me a better wife or friend.

Janet's Family

It is only right to mention that when I married Janet, I gained another set of grown children and grandchildren. I am pleased to have each one of them in my ever-increasing family.

Janet's oldest son, David Redding, is married to Nancy. He works for Frost Bank in Austin as a senior vice president of the financial management group. He and Nancy have two adorable girls, Victoria and Emma. They are tenderhearted and compassionate people, which led them to adopt two precious children from Ethiopia. One of the boys, Asher, is just three years old. His brother Levi is nine years old. They arrived early in 2009 and have already become U.S. citizens and much a part of the Redding family.

The second son is Scott. He is married to Kelly and they have three sweet daughters: Haley, Grace and Lottie. Scott is vice president of RPR Management, Inc., an investment management company.

Kristen, Janet's daughter, is married to Cody Stokes. They have a toddler named Landon who has just welcomed Tanner, a new little bother, into the world. Cody works for PBS&J; an architecture, construction, and engineering firm.

Fortune

One of the most significant things I ever heard pertaining to money came in a spiritual setting, before I ever had or lost much money.

Remember that stadium rally in St. Louis? The one I rented a bus for? Early on in that event, a woman got up to speak forth words I have not forgotten decades later. She spoke prophetically, as if the Lord himself were addressing the crowd.

"Oh man, why are you so concerned about money? Are you willing to see it blowing down the street, totally worthless? And yet, people are killing one another over it. I am going to destroy money and everything man is putting his faith in besides me."

Immediately, as she finished speaking, thousands of us rose from our seats as one and dropped to our knees. It was very clear to all of us that God had spoken and he wanted us to know his thoughts on this important subject. We remained humbled before Him. What is money compared to the Living God?

As for my personal experience over many years, I think I have gained a little of Paul's perspective. Paul, the apostle, said he knew the secret of being content with plenty or with little. I have experienced both. Many Christians in America think money is an answer to their troubles. I can assure you that money can be a dangerous trap. Scripture says, "The love of money is the root of all evil." When I go to Haiti, I marvel at the happiness of the people who have nothing while many in America, including myself, have chased after money to their own peril.

Most recently, we have seen the outcome of greed in the U.S. economic crisis, from the stock market to the housing market. The words I heard back in St. Louis come to my mind often. It is time for the people of faith to learn that secret of contentment. We are not to treasure what everyone else does, for no luxuries of this world compare to the treasure we have in Christ. I am reminded of Matthew 6:20-21. "But store up for yourselves treasures in heaven, where moth and rust do not destroy, and where thieves do not break in and steal. For where your treasure is, there your heart will be also."

A Time for Everything

Perhaps the only thing that can constrain us as much as money is time. That is one commodity we are all given equally. We each have a twenty-four hour day and must decide what we will do with it. When my daughter, Esta, wanted to delve seriously into art, she needed time to focus on what was important.

"I moved out to an old farm house in San Marcos, Texas," Esta says. "Dad gave me some wise words.

"He said, 'Esta, I know you will get lonely out there, but take advantage of this time alone and do not call your friends to come see you. There will come a time in your life where you will not be able to be alone. I would love to spend two weeks in

Colorado alone, but I can't. Take advantage of this opportunity.'

"So I did, and I painted up a storm. I did some of my best art. Beautiful stuff would appear on the canvas and I would wonder, how in the world did I do that?"

I know the outcome of the time and energy Esta spent there. I have some of her beautiful paintings hanging in my home.

How do we spend our time and our money? These are important resources we are given, and so these are significant questions to ask ourselves. How will I spend the time I am given today?

Fishing Lessons

I think fishing can be a great use of time. In fact, I think everyone should have a few chances over the course of life to enjoy fishing.

"I was not so good at fishing," says Gay, one of my lovely daughters. "When some people go fishing, it is about the whole experience on the water, or it's about taking someone with you and spending time. For Dad, the whole point is to catch fish, preferably many fish!

"I remember a recent time that Dad took Esta and me out to Lake Buchanan. There we were, adult women, and we did not catch a thing. Dad was determined. It was getting cold, and Esta and I were shivering in our coats at the bottom of the boat. I think we weren't taking the process too seriously, but Dad was. He saw birds dipping down and feeding in a spot across the water, so we had to go over to that spot. Sure enough, Dad caught a few fish, but as we tried to secure one of them, I dropped it back into the water! Esta and I began to laugh at this predicament. Dad did not see it as humorously as we did. I mean, his purpose was to be successful in getting the fish.

"Fishing tells me a great deal about Dad. His heart for his kids is just the same as his objective in fishing. He wants us to succeed. Whatever it is we determine to do, Dad's heart is for us to succeed."

Mary adds in, "As an adult, when I have had a tough day, Dad will say, 'Oh, honey, I am so sorry about that. Let me take you fishing.' It is his solution for those difficult moments."

Holy Communion

As much as I see fishing as a great way to gain perspective in life, there are some significant spiritual tools the Lord has given for our benefit: fellowship, prayer, and service being a few of them.

We build our lives on these foundations. I want to share with you the incredible experience I have had with another key component of the Christian faith, Communion.

Many years ago, about three o'clock in the morning, I was suddenly awakened from a sound sleep with a powerful awareness that God wanted to talk to me about the Lord's Supper. I had not been reading anything about the subject, nor had I been thinking about it at all. However, I knew without a doubt that He woke me and wanted to speak to me about it. I got out of bed, picked up a tablet and pen, and wrote the following as fast as I could write. I did not think about what to write, I just wrote as words came to me.

"Lord Jesus, what do you want to say to me about the Last Supper?"

"Herman, when one is about to die and knows it, the last thing he tells his friends and family is what he considers the most important of all the things he could talk about.

"Picture in your mind the scene in that Upper Room. I was with those I loved most in the world. What I shared with them was the very essence of My being and the central purpose of all I came to establish on earth.

"At that table, I was fully aware of the fact that on the morrow I would be giving My body as the God-ordained, ultimate sacrifice. My shed blood would provide the permanent and eternal Passover for all who would ever apply it. And yet, there is still much more.

"You and My church must pray for revelation knowledge of the fuller meaning. Paul received such knowledge, and I desire, yes, I implore you to seek that revelation knowledge for yourself and for My church in these latter days.

"As you seek to be one and to abide in Me and seek My face, you will come to realize how vital it is for you to enter in and fully partake of all I have made available to you through My mystical body and blood.

"It is here My body will be made one. It is here My bride will be perfected. Do not rest nor relax your search until My Spirit has revealed the fullness of all I have for you through this sacrament.

"This night, Herman, I am calling you to abandon all else in the search for the fullness I have for you and My church. Press in! Do not lose heart. What you find will be the greatest treasure that exists in heaven and on earth. I shall be with you. Trust Me. Look only to Me. This is vital to Me and to you."

Spirit Affecting Flesh

I pondered these words. Many of them are not words I would regularly use! Yet the Lord had me write those things down in the middle of the night. I know they are very important to Him, so they are important to me. The Lord confirmed to me the truth of His message in the days following.

I had hired a secretary about a week prior to this experience. I had not shared anything about it with her, yet only a few days later, she shared with me about a medical problem she had experienced for years. She had a chemical imbalance and had gone to all kinds of doctors with no results. One day God told her that He wanted her to quit seeing doctors, and every time she felt the symptoms returning, He wanted her and her husband to take Communion together. She followed these instructions.

"I am now totally healed," she said. Imagine! She obeyed, and by practicing Communion, a spiritual transaction occurred that brought healing to her physical body.

A sister in the faith from Haiti came to visit recently and joined us for the weekly prayer meeting in our home. She had suffered pain in her shoulders for several years due to an auto accident. She was healed in an instant that night as we took Communion together. Once again, I saw the powerful tool we have in Communion.

Our friend Larry, who spends much time before the Lord, is a survivor of four major heart attacks. We were greatly concerned when he was rushed to the Heart Hospital of Austin. Tests showed his heart and major arteries were severely blocked. Larry was scheduled for surgery, and Janet and I were able to serve him Communion before his operation. The medical team used a tiny camera to run through his arteries only to discover no blockage whatsoever. Upon his release, the lead doctor told him it was not legal to put on his record that a miracle occurred, so he wrote that there was a "mysterious disappearance."

Hearing and Grasping

Even as I saw physical miracles related to Communion, I pressed in to understand more fully what the Lord said to me. I went to the Bible and studied some of the difficult things Jesus said. I thought deeply on Jesus' words in John 6:53-58.

"Jesus said to them, 'I tell you the truth, unless you eat the flesh of the Son of Man and drink His blood, you have no life in you. Whoever eats My flesh and drinks My blood has eternal life, and I will raise him up at the last day. For My flesh is real food and My blood is real drink. Whoever eats My flesh and drinks My blood remains in Me, and I in him.'"

A few verses later, the passage says:

"On hearing it, many of His disciples said, 'This is a hard teaching. Who can accept it?' Aware that His disciples were grumbling about this, Jesus said to them, 'Does this offend you? What if you see the Son of Man ascend to where He was before! The Spirit gives life; the flesh counts for nothing. The words I have spoken to you are spirit and they are life.'"

More to the Message

I believe the miracles of healing show us that the Lord came to make us whole beings and that He uses Communion as one way to accomplish that. While we participate in the Lord's Table, He touches our brokenness and makes us well, in body and soul.

A second point to all of this is that we do it together. Through Communion I have access to God the Father, as well as unity with my brothers. We honor each other as fellow members of the Body of Christ when we join in Communion together.

The unity of all who believe in Christ, across denominations, races, and generations, is not taught much or acted upon. Yet, we are one Body. The Lord's Table becomes a meeting place; a common table where God and man come together; where we are made whole and we are made one.

The amazing thing about being made complete by God our Father and being unified with my brothers in faith, is that we are then free to serve others. Serving others is just what having a mission is all about.

Chapter Eleven
Hope for Haiti

So the poor have hope and
injustice shuts its mouth.
Job 5:16

I had recovered from a tragic car wreck. I had ventured to a foreign land, and now I had a new mission: getting solar cookers to Haiti. When I thought all hope of getting the cookers into Haiti was dashed, Mr. Veal at the U.S. Embassy had called, offering to expedite the import process. With that offer, I took my first trip to Haiti in the summer of 2000.

I was so captivated by the impoverished island nation that I have been there sixteen times in the last nine years. Yet I am hard pressed to paint an accurate picture of their poverty. There is despair, but there is also great hope and tangible joy in Haiti. I can tell you it is a tremendous blessing and a heart-touching challenge to hold a small, malnourished Haitian child in my arms. The frail body is a stark contrast to the tremendous potential I know dwells within that child.

Poorest of the Poor: Food for the Hungry

The statistics for Haiti are sobering. The average income has been reported at $400 a year. Some of the most recent reports say that, accounting for the tremendous inflation in Haiti, the figure is more accurately placed at $150. The country imports half of its food, and the average citizen spends most of their tiny income to purchase it.

Help for the Sick

A report issued by UNICEF says that Haiti has the highest death rate for children under five in the western world. The top two leading causes of death among children are preventable: diarrhea and pneumonia. Many of the problems stem from a lack of clean drinking water which affects as much as 80% of the population.

The consequences of these conditions became very real to me as one of my friends, Ginger Hammond, described her visit to a hospital in Cap Haitien. Cap Haitien is the second largest city in the country and serves as the capital for the region of Haiti known as the North Department.

For its prominence, Cap Haitien has very little to offer the sick. Ginger witnessed terrible conditions where the infirmed had to bring their own basic supplies. Sheets were not provided by the hospital, nor medicine. Not even electricity was available. Patients bring their own candles and food while family members try to buy medicine from any source they can. Imagine having to bring your own food or supplies to a hospital in the States!

Over the years, Janet and I have seen the effects left by diseases like TB and malaria. We have seen the children sick from intestinal worms. In many cases, just the fact that the children have no shoes continues to put them at risk for contracting another disease.

Perhaps the most compelling story is that of a little girl, no more than ten or eleven years old. Her mother brought her to a clinic while we were there. The mother reported that she had previously taken her sick child to a witch doctor. The girl became increasingly ill and began to vomit violently while waiting for treatment at the clinic. We are sad to say that the little girl died from her illness and the lack of adequate care right in front of our eyes. It was heartbreaking to see this unfold, and we knew it could not be an unusual event. How many more children go with inadequate care?

Education: Wisdom and The Word

The figures for education indicate more of the same. A little over half of the population enrolls in primary school, but by age ten, very few children remain in school.

Although public education is free, families must pay for uniforms, textbooks, and supplies. As a result private, schools with scholarships account for much of the education that is received. Yet with a significant drop out rate and a sizable population under age fifteen, it is estimated that only one in ten Haitians can read and write.

Over the years, I have been very pleased to support church schools for primary students and Bible schools for adults. It is clear that education is a vital tool for the people of Haiti in their battle against poverty. It is my deep desire not only to see that children can read and write, but that people know Christ and can study the Bible for themselves.

During that first trip in 2000, I was deeply touched. Beyond all the statistics and analysis, I knew that I had to help feed the people. I wanted to help make clean water accessible and support schools. I could clearly see the obstacles, but I also had a firm conviction that God would lead me to help make progress in Haiti.

Haiti's Call

I am, by far, not the only person greatly impacted by Haiti. One of the country's own, Wyclef Jean, has established a charitable organization to help the suffering children. Jean is an internationally known musician who left Haiti, made a fortune, and has returned to build clinics and raise scholarships to send children to school. He has reached out to the rich and famous in Hollywood to help publicize the great need in Haiti. Many relief organizations and charitable groups have been at work there for years. Much good has been accomplished, yet Haiti beckons for more.

Radical transformation

Perhaps no one has been so affected by Haiti's call as an amazing woman I have met, Susie Krabacher. Susie willingly tells her own story. Growing up as Susan Scott, she was an abused child who ran away as a teenager to seek her fortune as a Playboy centerfold. The many struggles that lead Susie down that path and the deception she saw in the world of glamour caused her to look for something more fulfilling. Susie was radically changed by faith in Jesus Christ and now works to help the poorest of the poor.

Susie is not just interested in Haiti's children. She is totally committed to them. She has taken on the task of long-term relief, reaching out to children in immediate need, but also making a difference in their future through health care centers and education.

Susie established The Mercy and Sharing Organization in 1994. Since that time she has raised literally millions of dollars to build schools, clinics and orphanages. Her efforts include an abandoned baby unit at a public hospital and two schools. One of the schools serves the sprawling slum of Cite Soleil, and the other is in the dangerous neighborhood of Cazeau. Susie has founded a clinic, established feeding programs, and raised funds for two orphanages, one for healthy children and one for disabled and terminally ill children. Most of Susie's children were abandoned by parents too poor to help them.

For some of the children Susie touches, it is too late. All she can do is provide little coffins with a note of love tucked inside as proof that someone cared for the little life that has now entered eternity. Although the need seems insurmountable, Susie is not deterred by the enormity of the task. She continues to work tirelessly; her faith is strong and her work effective. I am proud to know this servant of God.

My Story Continues: A Second Approach

Despite the appalling situation, I was so captivated by Haiti on my first visit that I wanted to do something significant, something that would bring real change. I left the solar cookers in good hands and pondered what more I could do. When I returned to the States, I drove to Colorado so I could pray and listen to the Lord's instructions.

Since I was headed through the Texas Panhandle, someone highly recommended that I stop in Lubbock to see Breedlove Dehydrated Foods Inc. It is an impressive operation. They supply dried food during natural disasters and send shipments for famine relief.

Typically, farmers in the U.S. have an excess of vegetables after filling their contracts with canneries. The surplus crops are usually plowed under, but the Breedlove Company has found ways to use that food for people in crisis. Farmers who donate their residual crops are granted a tax break. This is an amazing win-win situation. The farmers get a break, and the surplus, once dried, is easily stored and shipped. The meals have high nutritional value, yet cost about five cents each. Breedlove is a non-profit organization that can mobilize enormous quantities of food for foreign lands and for use in the U.S.

I was so impressed that I wanted to ship a quarter of a million meals to Haiti. Mr. Veal, my contact at the U.S. Embassy, was able to help once again. The container with two hundred and fifty thousand meals went directly through the Embassy to avoid the corrupt customs process. That supply of dried meals went to sixty schools and orphanages. The thank-you letters I received assured me that the meals made it to the children in need.

This seemed a new means for feeding the poorest in our half of the world. I set about sending a second shipment, but Kennedy Veal was no longer at the U.S. Embassy, and I was directed to use a non-governmental organization, or NGO. These organizations have the legal status to import goods to Haiti, custom free. Our shipment arrived in March, but was not sent on to the schools. The woman in charge of the NGO tried diligently to get the food out of customs, but months went by, and I grew very concerned. I knew the children were starving and that the meals had been stalled, unavailable to those in need.

Eventually the woman found that those holding up the process wanted a bribe. I confess, I paid the bribe. The meals were finally distributed in October. A seven-month delay, due to greed, was not an acceptable means of getting aid to the needy. This was a serious setback, but I could not relent. There had to be a way to help those precious people.

The Next Trip: Solar Power and Power of the Soul

I returned to the idea of solar cookers, but rather than shipping them, I wanted to look for a place to build them in Haiti. It takes $160 to build one in the States, plus the cost to ship it. I thought we might be able to build the devices there for much less. A Rotary Club in South Dakota heard of my interest in solar cooking, and we arranged a joint trip to Haiti.

Meanwhile, I was asked to participate on the Solar Energy Committee of Haiti. Our goal was to establish a self-sustaining village, using every means we could from solar cookers to a solar powered irrigation system. I met a few times with the committee, comprised mainly of Haitians, and the prospects were quite exciting. Good ideas were moving from the committee meetings to become useful tools in the field.

While in country with the Rotarians, I was invited to the North Haiti Mission in Caesse (Ky-ess), a small town near Trou-du-nord. The mission included a church and a school. It seems each time I go to Haiti, I find new connections and see how others are helping meet the needs of the people.

I have visited the North Haiti Mission, NHM, a half dozen times over the years. I helped construct a new school to replace the tiny little facility they had. Now the school serves 150 children who will not be added to the statistics of illiteracy. It is hard to grasp how excited the children are at the prospect of learning. They are pleased to crowd together on long benches. While school children in the U.S. seem to grow bored with school despite all our technology in the classroom, the children at NHM are happy simply to have paper and pencils and schoolbooks.

I also had the opportunity to help establish a medical clinic at NHM. Nurses staff the medical clinic in Caesse, while doctors come on a rotating basis. The clinic makes care more easily accessible for the local people and is a much better alternative than the poorly supplied hospital in Cap Haitien.

Martha and the Ovens

Through my involvement with the Solar Energy Committee, I was able to see some successes and also more of the obstacles Haiti faces. I visited a village with a well and an irrigation system totally run by solar power. However, the panels were at risk. The chronic poverty that the people face has prompted a mindset that says any resource can be taken. Although the solar power system worked, the panels were stolen.

Still, I talked about solar cookers any time I had the opportunity. One time when I explained the amazing value of this method, a woman in my church in Texas came to me to say she wanted to help. Martha Schultz introduced herself saying she did not know how to help in Haiti, but was willing to do so. She came along as part of the team on the next trip.

Since 2002, Martha has been thoroughly engaged with these ingenious devices. She has demonstrated solar ovens in North Haiti and has seen quite a response, especially from children. They are intrigued by the cookers! One of the mothers she met reports using the cooker the way women in the U.S. use crock pots: she places items in the solar oven in the morning and when she comes home, her dinner is ready. She doesn't need to watch or stir a pot over an open fire. A gentleman reports cooking many different kinds of food in his solar oven. Chicken, fish, rice, and vegetables, they all turn out well.

The ovens do not convey heat on the outside, even though the temperature on the inside reaches about 250 to 375 degrees. They are fiberglass, weigh ten pounds each and are stable in the wind. They are made by the Solar Oven Society in Minneapolis, Minnesota, a non-profit organization whose goal is to place these ovens in the hands of the poor. The Haitians spend about $150 each year on charcoal which kills the trees and represents a danger to children. Many children are burned when the parents cook on open fires and the smoke causes lung problems.

Yet, every time one of the solar ovens is used, a Haitian family saves the cost of buying charcoal, no smoke is produced, and another tree is spared. I am pleased to say that solar cooking has proven itself successful, and my hope is that the practice will spread across the entire nation. I am confident that if Martha has her way that is exactly what will happen.

An Effective Answer: Cooperative Gardens

On one of the trips, Janet and I walked through a very poor community to talk and pray for the people. We met a family on a Friday that said they had not eaten since Wednesday. I was deeply touched at the prospect of these parents telling their hungry children they had nothing to give them.

The economy is in ruins, and with tremendous unemployment, there is little hope for improvement. We saw that handouts are not the answer. They merely prompt an expectation for more and will not bring transforming change to Haiti. There must be a way to address the root causes, to put people to work and lead them to become self-sustaining. In November, 2008, Christianity Today published an article on world hunger. A gentleman from Africa is quoted:

"Give me the recipe. Do not just give me handouts. Give us the right type of missionary to empower our people to produce their own food." Although he speaks of Africa, I believe the same is true for Haiti.

On our third trip, I found an answer. We had the chance to see a cooperative vegetable garden, supported by a Canadian group in a little village not far from the North Haiti Mission called Terrier-

Rouge. The Canadians had helped establish a garden run by fifty Haitian families. It is so successful that all of the workers and their families are fed, and the surplus is sold at the market.

This concept is phenomenal, and the results truly amazing. It is life changing for the Haitians who have not had the opportunity to work. Gardening brings new skills and the dignity of work. Because these gardens are a cooperative effort, the families must appoint leaders who oversee each garden by committee. Unique in this leadership design, the gardens are also unique in their planting methods. Once the soil is prepared and the water supply is adequate, the seeds are planted very densely, unlike the single rows of crops we plant in the U.S. This method maximizes water use, yet does not deplete the soil and produces a much greater crop.

Lessons for Life

The establishing and running of a garden requires some level of skills. Often, a garden will be started in the poorest area where the vast majority of the people have not received any education whatsoever. The start-up cost for a coop garden includes a year's salary for an agronomist who must teach the people how to prepare the soil, plant the seed and how to tend the garden during the growing season while helping to establish the governing committees. The gardens are so much more than just food for the stomach. They offer a new way of life.

The leadership council for the garden Janet and I visited had devised a specific policy that works quite well. They return fifty percent of the profits to the members as cash, twenty-five percent to future garden expenses and twenty-five percent into a savings account for each family. This is a radical concept for the Haitians; they work, they eat, they sell the remaining crops, and they gain a tangible hope for the future. These gardens solve the issue of a handout that is consumed and immediately in need of replacement. Coop gardens can be maintained and produce a harvest as long as someone is willing to work. I think you could call cooperative gardening a sustainable miracle. I was so excited about this, I made it my mission to promote more gardens in Haiti.

Chapter Twelve
The Gardens Grow

Our First Garden

The Bible says: "If anyone has material possessions and sees his brother in need, but has no pity on him, how can the love of God be in him?" Janet and I had seen our brothers in great need, we had tremendous compassion and now we had a specific way to help.

We returned to Haiti, inspired by the Canadian group and their successful garden project. We were able to lease five acres next to the North Haiti Mission. We knew the process would take several steps to complete, and that some serious obstacles had to be overcome. We needed adequate land and water as well as a way to teach the people to prepare, plant and manage the garden.

Soil, Seed and Security

Suitable and available land is just the start. The land must be plowed to turn the soil. Often the plow must make three passes to dislodge the rocks and turn up the topsoil at a deep enough level to be effective. Then the rocks have to be removed, which may not seem a great task in the U.S. where the right equipment can be obtained. However, in Haiti few tools are available. Much of the work is done by hand, making this no small job for five acres.

With the land prepared, we needed the right type of seeds to plant. For that we turned to Hope Seeds, a faith-based organization out of Florida that is quite knowledgeable about agricultural practices all over the world. I like the fact that their Biblical directive goes all the way back to Genesis. You can see God's provision from the very beginning in Genesis 1:29: "I have given you every plant with seeds on the face of the earth and every tree that has fruit with seeds. This will be your food." It is a fact that God's provision is great, if we know how to help people gain it.

Security is one more issue for the newly established garden. Animals and humans both pose a threat, so there is a real need for adequate fencing. Once the land is secured, there is an essential factor for growth.

Working Water

The next obstacle is accessible and clean water. Unsanitary water is an enormous issue in Haiti. It is reported that over thirty percent of the youngest children do not survive due to the lack of clean water. That is one of those statistics that is simple enough to read, but incredibly hard to grasp. Nearly a third of the infants and small children die, simply because they do not have an adequate, clean water supply.

An added cruelty to the water issue is the location of supplies. Water is often hauled long distances by children and women. Anyone who has carried a bucket for a distance knows that water is heavy. We heard of a pregnant woman who lost her baby because of the strenuous work of hauling water. We have seen for ourselves how small children carry plastic buckets and jugs full of water from a distant source back to their village. We had to get clean water to the people and near enough to the gardens.

As Janet and I investigated, we found that some water wells existed, but needed repair. Other cases required drilling new wells. For our first 5-acre project, we hired a gentleman to drill a new well for us. We were on our way, not only to a new garden, but to understanding the wonderful people and ministries that have areas of expertise that could help us accomplish our goal. Water wells are a double blessing because the wells that serve the gardens also provide the community with clean drinking water. We accomplish a great deal with this one precious commodity; the families gain safe water and the gardens flourish.

One of the groups that came to our attention is Living Water International, a Christian organization serving the poorest communities in the world. They work to meet physical and spiritual needs at the same time. Their literature says it simply: "LWI exists to demonstrate the love of God by helping communities acquire desperately needed clean water, and to experience 'living water'—the gospel of Jesus Christ—which alone satisfies the deepest thirst."

Janet and I soon heard about Bill Houk who worked with LWI on a well repairing team in Haiti. He now serves through a branch of LWI called Living Water Midwest. Since then we have worked together with Bill to see the garden projects become a reality in Haiti. We are glad to report that when 10 wells were repaired, some forty thousand people received the benefits of a clean, local water supply.

Bill was a key person in the acquisition of a new tractor that has been sent to Haiti to help drill more wells. This beautiful piece of equipment is a blue, 95 horsepower, four wheel drive, New Holland tractor. Living Water International has graciously added a drilling rig to the tractor. The rig, already mounted and ready, has a diamond drill bit that should conquer just about anything we hit in our search for water. It may sound odd, but I think miracles can come in the form of heavy machinery, and I am very happy about this one in particular.

The Cooperative Part

Organization and cooperation are key elements in this garden effort. It may seem obvious to people in the U.S. that any group needs leadership, but the Haitians have had little say in many charitable efforts within their own country. This is a significant flaw and must be addressed if the people are to sustain themselves. A sense of ownership is vital.

To participate in a cooperative garden, the people must work, and they must provide a leadership committee from among themselves. Those leaders take on the job of assigning tasks and providing accountability, and they make decisions regarding profits from the surplus harvest sold at the market. This is another place for the lead agronomist hired for each garden to teach the people not just planting skills, but how to work together.

Feeding the Soul

Make no mistake; our desire to serve in Haiti is prompted by our faith in Christ who calls on us to serve the poor. We know that we must feed the souls of the people, or our task is incomplete. Because many people in Haiti have never heard the Gospel and cannot read, we seek to give them an opportunity to hear the message of Jesus Christ in Haitian Creole.

We work with Faith Comes by Hearing, an organization that provides a device called a Proclaimer. It is an audio player programmed with the New Testament in a community's native language. It can run on one of multiple energy sources, such as solar power or a hand crank. We are committed to getting a Proclaimer for every community with a cooperative garden. To gain the greatest impact with these amazing little machines, the local pastors arrange for "listening groups" to come together regularly to hear the Bible.

"Converted"

We believe with absolute certainty that reaching the soul is critically important and prompts great changes. When a Haitian comes to faith in Christ, they refer to the process as conversion. They understand that the new Christian will think, act and live differently than they did before. It is very clear when a person converts from the realm of darkness to the light and knowledge of Christ.

Perhaps no clearer picture of this conversion experience can be seen than in a gentleman I have met who once served as a voodoo priest in a remote village. Although he was at first resistant to hearing about Jesus Christ, he experienced God's great compassion and was literally transformed in a divine moment. He went so far as to grant permission to burn his voodoo paraphernalia to insure he would never use it again. This man is no longer the threatening person he once was. Now he radiates joy, peace and love; all because he received the love of God into his soul.

Haiti Gardens

We believe so deeply in the benefits of coop gardens that we established a non-profit organization in 2005 called Hope for Haiti, Inc.

We spent quite a bit of time coordinating efforts to bring the gardens from a good concept to reality. We promoted the cause, publicized the work, and began receiving donations. We found that to hold tax-exempt status, we needed a governing Board of Directors and an Advisory Board, which meant contacting many people and pulling them together. The Lord brought us some amazing people to sit on both of our boards who are knowledgeable and quite well qualified.

However, we found that running a non-profit organization, traveling to Haiti, learning more about tackling hunger, and then handling donations was more than we could do. We needed help with the daily administrative duties and financial record keeping. There is a serious need among non-profits to be honest and accountable, and we wished to do both well. Although we needed help, Janet and I were not about to hand over the responsibilities of money handling to just anyone. We asked my daughter, Donna, for help, and she said we needed an executive director. She devised a job description that detailed the person and qualities we were looking for.

Hope for the Hungry

With our interest in fighting hunger, we are directed toward all sorts of groups that share a similar vision. So it is not terribly surprising that we were told about a group fighting world hunger. What is amazing is the quality of people the Lord has brought our way. We heard about Hope for the Hungry, HFH, a non-profit organization that happens to be located in Belton, Texas, not far from us. We learned that they were offering a five day mission school so we signed up to attend the training. There we got to know the founder of HFH, Dan Kirkley, and his assistant C.J. Rich. We were very impressed with their compassionate hearts for Haiti.

HFH was established in 1982 and has experience serving the poor in many nations. We were so pleased to find they were already working in Haiti where they have established orphanages for boys and girls. These children have grown up to be very godly people and are now making an impact on their own nation.

Some months later, we set up a meeting with Dan and C.J., hoping to get direction for our ministry. When Dan read through Donna's description of what we needed in a director, tears came to his eyes.

"I believe the Lord is saying we should provide this for you," he said. Janet and I were ecstatic.

As members of the ECFA, the Evangelical Council for Financial Accountability, Hope for the Hungry holds to the highest standards, including financial audits. Any donor can request a financial statement and see just how the funds are used. Every cent donated to Hope for the Hungry goes to the field, according to Dan. The staff members raise their own support and thereby do not draw from donated funds for their own administrative positions, which is nearly unprecedented. Almost every charity draws some funding from donations for administration, but not so with Hope for the Hungry. We were impressed by this practice, and we were even more encouraged by their offer to handle the finances for our projects in Haiti. We are very honored to have Dan serving on our Hope for Haiti Board of Directors.

We are blessed to see how our vision for cooperative gardens has led us to people who can help with clean water, with the Word of God, and with financial oversight. Our program would not be successful without each of these components. We see how the Lord has supplied them all.

Learning More, Planting More

When I say Janet and I are directed to resources, people, and organizations, I mean it. Hardly a week goes by that we don't learn about another group doing something that affects world hunger.

In 2005, we had a call from a friend who heard about a trip to Swaziland planned by Bruce Wilkinson's Heart for Africa organization. They were sending 350 volunteers to start up private home gardens for 10,000 families, so Janet and I jumped at the chance to go along. We had Eddie Francois, our pastor friend from Haiti, join us so we all could learn firsthand how this large-scale operation was handled.

To jump start the program, they used seedlings, or small plants, instead of seeds. The land was prepared in advance, and the seedlings were held in green houses so the volunteers could come in with a streamlined operation and plant as much as possible. In a very short period of time, 10,000 families had gardens in place! It was an amazing feat that we hope can be duplicated someday in Haiti.

Growing Success

Our first garden was so successful that we helped start six more. The smallest garden sustains thirty-five families, but most of them provide for fifty. This means that men, women, and children all have enough vegetables to eat and a surplus to sell from just five acres of soil. We began by leasing land, but we have found that in many cases, churches already own land or the members of their congregations do. Now we have requests from more churches wishing to establish coop gardens on their land.

Hope for Haiti is looking for individuals and churches that wish to support new gardens. Without paying to lease land, the start-up costs for a new garden are about $11,000 for the first year. Those funds cover every component: the preparing of the soil, water wells, secure fencing, tools, seeds, and a year's salary for an agronomist to teach the people. The cost is significantly less the second year, and hopefully, the gardens will be self-sustaining after that. I believe that cooperative gardens will be a tremendously important tool in transforming Haiti into a nation that can feed itself.

Stones to Cabbages

We have seen firsthand the transformation the land undergoes. In December of 2007, Janet and I visited a church property that had been selected for a garden. We had donated funds for the wells to be drilled. The people had attempted to plow the ground with a tractor, but it broke down. After that, they used a cow to do the plowing, but I would have to say it was not very promising. Big clods of dirt protruding from the ground left me wondering just what they could produce with clumps of dirt and their meager equipment.

Janet and I returned less than three months later to a lush garden flourishing with green leaves and vegetables! The size of the vegetables the land produces is really quite amazing. These precious Haitian people wanted to celebrate the success of their garden with us, I suppose as a thank you for our involvement. They had a table prepared under a tree where they served us Coca-Cola. Here they were, treating us to a luxury, yet all the while it was our desire to help them. The success of the garden was more satisfying than the cool soda on a warm day.

Trusting Wisely

On occasion, you might hear someone use the phrase, "take the money and run." Until recently, I would not have said that this was a common expression referring to business practices in the U.S. But it is not unusual in Haiti because of the extreme poverty. As I said before, debilitating poverty over decades warps the thinking.

We had the unpleasant task of firing the top two agronomists we had hired. These gentlemen were believed to be reliable as well as knowledgeable about agriculture, and they were paid to instruct the coop garden members. Yet money disappeared under their watch. As troubling as our predicament was, we have heard much worse from Susie Krabacher and others who attempt to do good works in Haiti. We learned the hard way that it is essential to investigate partners and any ministry before we invest. It is my pledge to make Hope for Haiti as honest and successful as possible. People with integrity are essential to that goal.

Wilbert and Meg

Janet and I had met Wilbert Merzilus on one of our many trips to Haiti, and in late 2008, we reconnected. He came very highly recommended, and I can see why. Wilbert is probably the wisest Haitian man I have ever met.

About fifteen years ago, Wilbert and his wife Meg founded Living Hope Mission Ministries, Inc. Wilbert grew up poor on a farm in northern Haiti. His sister paid for his early education. Later, Wilbert got to finish his secondary education in Cap-Haitien and then attend college in the States when a family friend in the U.S. offered to pay for it. His wife Meg is from Ohio. After college, she worked on the mission field in an orphanage and taught English at a Haitian vocational school.

Together, they help independent churches in rural Haiti, working to affect the body, the mind and the soul. They have opened Hope Center where young people, parents, farmers, church leaders, and preachers can learn through a series of formal and informal classes. Along with their staff, they teach ways to improve agricultural practices or provide better animal care, and they give instruction on practical details such as how to establish a fishpond. Recently, their mission began providing nutrition and health classes for children in rural schools. Things that you or I might think logical or take for granted have to be taught in Haiti. The people have to be wise, as their resources are few.

Living Hope Mission Ministries works with twelve churches that run or support ten schools where hundreds of children benefit from their tuition assistance programs. In most of the schools, the children receive a hot lunch of rice and beans every school day, which for most of them is the only meal for the day. Once again, it has been my pleasure to see the smiling faces of many children, excited about their chance to learn.

Yet, that opportunity does not come free. Wilbert knows that Haitians value what they invest in. Even the poorest parents must pay something toward their children's education, and if they absolutely cannot pay anything, they are asked to come work at the school, perhaps to sweep the floors. Everyone who benefits must contribute. Wilbert is insistent on this policy because he knows it works. He and Meg are valuable assets to their community and are highly respected. We are so thankful God has brought us together.

The Pilot Project

Wilbert and Meg have supported the development of vegetable gardens and encouraged families to participate. Wilbert has been offered 160 acres for large-scale garden projects. Hope for

Haiti has started a joint venture with Living Hope Mission due to his expertise. Of the 160 acres, 25 were set aside for a Pilot Project that is profit-based. Under Wilbert's direction, ninety-eight people have been hired part time to work the land. The crops will be sold at the market and the proceeds will go to the schools supported by Living Hope Mission. There are very careful accounting measures and oversight standards in place.

I am excited about this Pilot Project as it draws together many of the techniques and principles we have learned through our previous cooperative gardens. It also addresses the need for employment. Those who gain a salary from the work, as well as others in the community, will benefit from the harvest. By God's grace, this Pilot Project could lead to much larger gardens, employing many Haitian people while supplying much-needed food.

With this project and our successful family gardens, we may have found a viable solution to many of the ills that plague Haiti's poor. We are encouraged as we see many components coming together to tackle the issues of poverty and hunger. Robert Zachrist of World Vision says that the answer to hunger will be a corporate one.

"We need good governments. We need businesses. We need the Church, the faith-based community. We need big NGOs (non-governmental organizations). We need smaller NGOs. If you look at Bill Gates, he cannot solve this by himself. The Church cannot solve this by itself. We need to work together. Where you get synergy, that's where you develop the answers."

The Mission Continues

The Lord has brought another well-qualified couple our way: Dennis and Jennifer Maupin from Clinton, Missouri. They are in the process of moving from the U.S. to the northern part of the island where they will serve as long term missionaries. The Maupins come to Hope for Haiti with international experience, having participated in many mission trips early in their marriage and then serving in east Africa from 1995 to 2001.

Dennis knows his way around a construction site as well as how to lead Bible classes. He has recently directed Powell Gardens, a not-for-profit botanical garden near Kansas City, Missouri, covering more than 900 acres. Jennifer is a teacher with experience in public and private schools. Most of all, they have a tender heart toward the poor in Haiti. The Maupins will help facilitate water projects and establish more gardens in connection with Living Water Midwest and Hope for Haiti.

I believe we are poised on the edge of something transformational. We continue to stand back in amazement as we see God bringing people and ministries together. He touches hearts with His compassion and we are united in our mission to serve the poor. May the Lord bless our work in Haiti and all who help us, so that together, we may see a vast harvest in the gardens and in His Kingdom.

Epilogue

"WHAT YOU DO FOR THE LEAST OF THESE YOU DO FOR ME."
MATTHEW 25:40

I am about to turn eighty-five years old. I have made sixteen trips to Haiti, and I hope to make many more, God willing. I do not take credit for my health or my opportunity to do this work. The Lord has given it all. Because God has woven my life together, it is fitting that I worship Him and serve Him.

He protected me in my early days, through the war years and through two car wrecks. He allowed me to experience being hungry, so that I would have compassion for those who suffer in the same way. He led me through my education, even giving me a keen interest in agriculture, which adds to my interest in the gardens in Haiti.

Now I wish to extend the challenge to others to walk with God the Father, honor Jesus the Son, and listen for the guiding of the Holy Spirit. Look around our world. There are plenty of needs and few willing workers. I think I am proof that you cannot be too young or too old to be effective. No one is disqualified from taking up a mission.

For the young people who may have read this book, I want to say that you do not have to graduate from high school or college to be ready to serve God. If you have heard my story, you know that I helped my family at a very young age. I worked for the benefit of my high school before I left for the Navy.

The challenge you face may not be your own personal hunger, but I ask you to find out what the needs are around you. You live in a connected society. Learn about your world and the needs in it, and I am sure you will find a place to serve. There are many people in need of help. Venture out. Take the mission trip. See the poor. There are more of them than there are of us.

A word to the senior citizens: please do not waste your "golden years." I know you have worked hard and want to enjoy life while you can. Is retirement a good thing? Some studies show it is not. Not for those who disengage from life. We are made by our Creator for a purpose -- destined for a mission -- if you will. Your service to God may look quite different from mine, but you still need to serve. Think of all the many things you have learned over your long life. Take stock of your interests, training, and talents, and do not put them to rest. Employ them now, for we are all called to make a difference. You were given these gifts on purpose. I am asking you not to coast to a stop, but to finish well. As you do this, my prayer is that our mighty and all-powerful God will send you on a mission, whether to Haiti or next door.

Once again, I will ask each reader to take my hand and join me in planting gardens in Haiti. You can go physically or in your heart. Either way, you can serve the starving children there. Remember, Jesus said, "What you do for the least of these you do for me." In a way, you have already begun to help Haiti's poor, because every penny of profit from the sale of this book goes to Hope for Haiti. You can go another step by encouraging others to purchase a book.

A step beyond that is giving regularly. If you wish to give to Hope for Haiti, we would be greatly honored to use your dollars to grow more gardens. Even a few dollars a month can make a difference. I pray that God will multiply back to you a hundred times as much as you give to poor, hurting people. A giant step for some might be visiting that amazing country yourself. I warn you that it is captivating!

Hope for Haiti offers the opportunity to travel there and see firsthand the wonderful things God is doing. Come, see our gardens and meet the precious people.

Now for the most important question of all. I ask you to join me on another trip, this one for eternity. Do you know, for certain, where you will spend it? Life on this Earth is quite short compared to all of eternity. If you have not ever done so, I encourage you to give your life to Jesus, ask Him to forgive all your sins, which He will do. Then, you and I will be together in heaven forever with Him.

While we are on this side of heaven, what a journey this life of faith is! As the Haitians say we are "converted," changed and made new. I want to stress how very important it is after conversion to spend time regularly in God's Presence. When we worship Him and study His Word, we listen to God and become more obedient to Him. If we do this, He will use us in amazing ways. I know this to be true. I have told you of my own experiences while hunting in Colorado when the Lord blessed me because I chose to worship Him and put Him first.

Remember my friend Larry Stokes? He spends hours every day before the Lord, and as a result, he has drawn very close to God and has benefited from many miracles. Supernatural things happen around Larry on a regular basis. I believe that is due to his personal closeness with God, the Father.

I believe that if you will invest time in worshipping Christ and listening to His voice, He will use you mightily as well. Jesus said, "Greater things than I have done you will do because I am going to the Father." Time in God's Presence is the most profitable way to spend the valuable commodity He has given us.

Please come and join me in this incredible journey of faith because our mission is made possible through His power.

How to Donate to Hope for Haiti and Garden Projects

Hope for Haiti, Inc. - www.haitigardens.org

Hope for Haiti is a Texas based non-profit 501(c)(3) organization. Donations should be made to:

> Hope for the Hungry
> P.O. Box 786
> Belton, Texas 76513

Please attach a note specifying the gift is for Hope for Haiti.

Websites of Interest

Breedlove - www.breedlove.org

Faith Comes By Hearing - www.faithcomesbyhearing.com

Hope for the Hungry - www.hopeforthehungry.org

Hope Seeds - http://hopeseeds.org

Living Hope Mission Ministries, Inc. - www.livinghopemission.org

Living Water Midwest - www.livingwaterinternationalmidwest.org

Susie Krabacher - www.haitichildren.com

Acknowledgements

From Herman and Janet Neusch

We wish to thank Dan Davis, not only for having the idea for this book, but also for finding our very competent and dedicated author, Kathy Glover. She was a joy to work with. Thank you, Kathy, for hanging in there with us.

We also thank our family and prayer group for encouragement through this process and for their prayer support over many months.

Janet and I want to acknowledge the Board of Directors for Hope for Haiti, Inc. We are so very grateful to the Lord and to the wonderfully talented people He has brought our way to serve the poor in the name of Christ. The members of our Board are:

Herman Neusch, Cofounder
Janet Neusch, Cofounder and Secretary
Bill Neusch, President
Don Barlow, Vice President
Dan Kirkley, Treasurer
Anne Holland
Bill Houk
Dick Rudman
Robert St. George
Joe Schultz
John Williams

Bill Neusch

You have met Bill in the pages of this book. He has been in the fence business since 1984 and runs a group of companies known as the Gibraltar Family of Businesses. In August of 2008, Bill felt God calling him to work with Herman and the garden projects in Haiti. Three days later we asked him if he would consider taking over the presidency of Hope for Haiti. He knew it was God's timing and will and has been a great asset to our ministry since then. He has leadership qualities and business experience that we needed in our organization and he definitely has a heart for missions.

Don Barlow

Don and his wife Julie are volunteers for the American Red Cross and go at a moment's notice wherever they are called. Don and Julie have both been trained to repair water wells in Haiti and have been there several times. Don has served on our board since the beginning of our ministry.

Dan Kirkley

Dan is the treasurer of Hope for Haiti and is the founder of Hope for the Hungry in Belton, Texas. Once again, we thank him for his devotion to Christ and to the poor. We are honored to have him serve with us.

Anne Holland

Anne lives in Fort Worth, Texas, where she is President and CEO of Mayco Oil. She is a woman of great influence with her own unique and amazing story. Anne grew up quite poor in a Ukrainian family in rural Canada. When she came to the U.S., she worked her way up through a corporate travel business where she made contacts in the crude oil marketing industry. Anne changed businesses, and although she enjoyed great success, she found her spiritual life lacking. After a serious search, Anne came to Christ, and now she is committed to serving others through several Christian organizations. She has great passion for the poor and is an asset to our board.

Bill Houk

Bill is from Missouri and serves on our Board of Directors as well as the board for Living Water Midwest. In 2005, Bill had been working on water wells in Central America when he had an opportunity to repair wells in Haiti. Herman invited him to attend one of our board meetings and he saw the importance of water for our garden projects. Bill encouraged his church in Clinton, Missouri, to get involved. He and Robert St. George conduct training camps on drilling water wells so many will be able to go and serve. Bill was a key player in getting the new tractor and drilling rig that has been shipped to Haiti. Robert and Bill are coordinating teams to drill many wells there.

Dick Rudman

Dick has served on our board of directors since the beginning. He is a retired Southwest Airlines pilot with a background in farming and a degree in agriculture. He says, "I was greatly inspired by Herman's vision to help the people of Haiti." Dick's educational background is a wonderful help to us in our garden projects.

Robert St. George

Robert is from Missouri and currently serving on the Board of Directors for Hope for Haiti and for Living Water

Midwest. Beginning in 1973, he served eight years in the U.S. Marine Corps as an air traffic controller. From 1982-2005 he worked in the Kansas City Center as an enroute air traffic controller. He is currently employed by the Mitre Corporation. It is a federally funded research and development corporation. He is a contract engineer to re-design and evaluate air space. He adds insight and wisdom to our board.

Joe Schultz

Joe has owned his own construction business for twenty-two years. He is a very talented builder and has been to Haiti several times, using his experience to help the Haitians build a medical clinic and a school. Joe's heart is for missions, specifically in Haiti.

John Williams

John and his wife, Donna, have been to Haiti several times and they desire to help the Haitian people in any way they can. They own a lodge on Lake Buchanan, Thunderbird Resort, which they rent for family outings, retreats and meetings. They are constantly serving others. John led the team that went to Haiti in July, 2009.

We would also like to take this opportunity to thank our Advisory Board for their service to the people of Haiti as well. We are grateful to them for the insight they bring to Hope for Haiti. Our current members are: Ginger Hammond, Don Herrington, John Ingle, Buddy Jungman and Martha Schultz.

Acknowledgements

From Kathy Glover

I would like to thank my partners in prayer at Northwest Fellowship: MaryAnne Kent, Linda Lyon, Kathie Miller and Cynthia Wyman. My thanks also goes out to Angela Bolton for reading the earliest pages of this manuscript and encouraging me. I am grateful to Angela Dolbear for her expertise with photographs and her diligent efforts to place them well. I would also like to thank Michelle and Robert Bauman for pointing out the absolute necessity of designated writing space. The prayers and insight of these people helped make this book a reality.

About the Author

Kathy Glover lives in Central Texas with her husband, Danny. They have a daughter, Shelby, and a son, Shannon, who are both in college. The Glovers attend Northwest Fellowship and share a passion for prayer and small groups. Kathy has a Radio-TV-Film degree from The University of Texas at Austin. She loves words, especially when woven together to tell an enlightening story.